Life in the Slow Lane

A patient quest for adventure

Dave Cornthwaite

Sleeve photography © Dave Cornthwaite
Front cover: the author reclines with a tortoise

Rear cover (clockwise from top left):
Sailing the Pacific with the Pangaea Explorations
scientific yacht, Sea Dragon.

The final salute from the Wolf River, as the paddlers
approach Mud Island at the end of the journey.

Priscilla the Bikecar parked up on Santa Rosa Island,
Florida, with the Gulf of Mexico in the background.

davecornthwaite.com

ISBN: 1490570888
ISBN-13: 978-1490570884

Amazon Reviews

"Dave Cornthwaite's ethos is to "say yes more", to make every moment and every opportunity count. That ethos comes to life in the pages of his latest book, which is as engaging as it is thought-provoking."

"Reflective, comical and love-strewn, this is a story about living free. A glow-in-the-dark adventure that will make you smile."

"A gentle pace that draws you in without you realising."

"For anyone who has had those moments of `what if I just walked away from what is expected and chose to do what I want instead?' I defy you to read it and not finish thinking that you really should get off your arse and just DO something."

"His latest work does not disappoint. Funny and engaging."

"Refreshing! Honest! Inspiring! Genuine! Different! Uncomplicated and Sincere! A truly original approach to Adventure and personal challenges."

"Unparalleled patience, empathy, tolerance, lots of humour, buckets of will-power and self-determination sprinkled with the flavour of a flourishing romance."

"You just cannot go through the summer without reading this book. Funny, touching, brilliant."

"What Dave shares quite eloquently is that maybe, just maybe, his is the real world, with most people living in a world that…how can I put it… isn't what real life should be."

"Eloquent and witty; bursting with enthusiasm and positivity. Even if you're already reasonably fulfilled, this book is a warm reminder that you're on the right track and should keep going. If you're not one of these people and you're in a rut, this book is a helpful little nudge up the ladder. You don't need to be an adventurer to enjoy this - it's as much about life as anything else."

Other books by Dave Cornthwaite

BoardFree (2008)

Two weeks after Dave Cornthwaite tried riding a long skateboard for the first time, he woke up and made the biggest decision of his life. BoardFree is the story of one man's extraordinary determination to escape a rut.

Within two years Dave taught himself how to skate, quit his job, set up a charitable initiative, then embarked on two incredible skateboard journeys to raise money and awareness for three charities. He pushed the length of Britain and the width of Australia, breaking two world records and inspiring many others to go on and do something similar.

Date (2011)

When Dave Cornthwaite decided to find a girlfriend by attempting to date 100 women in 100 days, the result was an emotional rollercoaster that threatened to turn his world inside out and upside-down. He searched high and low, online and on the street. Encountering awkward embraces, inappropriate foot rubs and an unexpected dose of heartache, Dave's latest journey proved that even with the best of intentions, finding love can be the hardest challenge of all…

A revealing insight into the way men think and act on the dating scene, DATE is the hilariously candid story of one man's struggle to get to the bottom of this crazy little thing called love.

The Author

Dave Cornthwaite is a record-breaking adventurer, author and motivational speaker. He was once quite a bad graphic designer, but outside of work hours was a total whizz on any games console you care to mention. Eventually, recognising that he only had so many brain cells left to lose, he decided to pursue a new career doing something he enjoyed, which strangely had been a life path not much encouraged throughout his education.

Dave's Expedition1000 project is recognised as one of the most ambitious adventures around. At the time of publishing he had completed eight from a series of twenty-five journeys, each at least 1000 miles in distance, each using a different form of non-motorised transport.

Dave is also the founder of Say Yes More, an organisation designed to encourage people to love their work and make the most of their time on this lovely planet of ours. The key is quite simple; he just wants you to say yes more.

Find out more at www.davecornthwaite.com

Chapters

EP, how much of this book is for you?

I'll give you a clue. More than a little bit.

x

1

Impact

From the soles of my feet it spread without pause, through and beneath and across the surface of my skin in every direction: hungry wildfire, uncontrollable, preparing my body for the worst.

Death at its most dramatic fails to approach quietly. South America: the groan of an ageing truck losing its natural trajectory before plummeting over the edge, silent releases of air from everyone on board aware of the inevitable. Western Australia: my friend's uncontrollably sad, guttural wails upon learning of a loved one's death, a black telephone at her feet when we reached her. Kenya: a sigh of resignation of a mother horizontal on a dirty mattress in her final moments, ridden with disease and heartbreak. Uganda: the soft, theatrical buzz of a bullet through the air, then a sickening, surprising thud as its journey ends in a human being. Then screams.

This scream was different. Intimidating. Inescapable. Haunting. I reacted to the plague of realisation instinctively, tensing my muscles, gripping the handlebars. I thought of *her*, then calculated the likely chain of events that were unfolding out of sight behind me, and braced.

The departure of time gains pace in response to one treating it with contempt. It may have been one, two or five seconds between the woman realising that she was about to collide with the van in front of her and the momentary physical stillness at the roadside that would follow, but I remember a countless number of my own thoughts from that period. Life didn't flash before my eyes, rather, the possibilities of how it could end wrapped around the moments I would never experience if this finished badly. Judging by the sound of burning, out of control tyres that chased us down the highway, Hell lay in wait.

Knuckles white, I reverted to my natural state and became simple. I was staring forwards towards the southeast so my understanding of the event was not through sight, just imagination and sense. I traced the threatening arc of sound from directly behind, and then to the left and suddenly back again, but an explanation of this pattern I couldn't process. There was clearly a vehicle in desperation back there, and the first crumpling of metal against metal confirmed a hunch that our support vehicle would be struck. From the very start I had prepared for this, assuming that following a collision Dale and his van would adopt the speed of the suspect car behind then in turn race forwards into us.

As every potential consequence charged through my mind the option of not being hit didn't appear on the list. Surely we were next. Myself, Rod, Priscilla the Bikecar: the last obstacle in line, it was just a matter of time.

And then it *was* our turn. Impact.

2

Let the Seed Grow

Luck is a positive result of chance; if you don't give yourself a shot at chance luck is less likely to find you. Bad luck doesn't have the same rules as good luck: it can pay you a visit at the most unnecessary of times and all you can do is deal with it. If you're the type of person to open yourself up to chance, my best guess is you'll be well suited for a speedy recovery, whatever life throws at you.

2011 met 2012 in a haze of potential and delightful uncertainty. I had no plans for the year ahead yet still felt it was going to be one of my most productive. I'd just experienced a pretty hefty yet typical slump in motivation following what was the most enjoyable expedition of my life but spirits were slowly lifting. Options to create a new move arrived in my inbox by the hour, and I hadn't had a proper job in about seven years. Apart from the small and temporary question of post expedition blues, life was just about as perfect as it could get.

I think we have two flat choices in life. Follow the herd

or follow your heart. Exist, or evolve. I had sucked at school, taken a gap year in East Africa, gone to University without having a clue about what I should study, then backpacked and hitchhiked a bit but always came home without answers. I bought a house when I was twenty thanks to terraces in South Wales costing similar to a shed in London, but then I had bills to pay, which meant I had to work despite being too young for life experience to inform me of my natural path. One day I woke up unhappy and realised the only difference between then and any of the days, weeks, months and years beforehand was that I was now aware of how I felt, rather than accepting monotony as normal.

It's a bit of a blow, lying in bed with a partner of three years who had allowed no physical activity beyond spooning for six months. It's damaging to the confidence, and gingers don't need any help with that, we're already a minority. My weekdays were spent in an office designing newspapers that people didn't read and advertisements for products that nobody in their right mind would buy. And they were crap designs. I couldn't even take pride in the superficial creative element, because the end result was useless. I did a job because it paid me money, because someone paid the company money, in order for someone else to pay them money. For nothing. No real value. No real pride. Just money. I hated myself for being a part of that pointless economic circle and then I went home and played a Playstation for hours so I wouldn't have to talk to the girlfriend. There wasn't a single element of my life that made me happy, except for Kiwa the cat. Tick, tick, tick. Death had come early.

The average life expectancy for someone in the western world is about 80 years old, yet for no apparent reason we determine our quarter-life crisis to arrive at 25. The promise of living to the beautifully simple age of 100 teases us out of reality. Silly us, we think we're going to work until we're 60 and then have 40 whole years of fun when in all probability, there are just 20 left.

This ran through my mind on the morning of my 25th birthday and stewed for about half a year before breaking point, upon which I decided that when someone asked me what I did for a living I'd endeavour to be proud of the answer, rather than mumble under my breath, 'I'm a graphic designer. You know, it, erm, pays the mortgage.'

So I did something new. I took up longboarding and saw the world in a different way just because I was riding around it in a *different way*. Two weeks later I quit my job. A year later I became the first person to skateboard the length of Britain. Two months after that I flew to Australia and spent five months pushing my board across that large, empty, wonderful country. I'd been ridiculed, warned and berated but not one of the reasons people offered in their attempt to protect my safety proved to be adverse. The most important lesson I learned from skateboarding four and a half thousand miles was that human beings can only offer an opinion based on what *they* would do. And as of that moment in mid January 2007, skating through the streets of Brisbane, Queensland, having undertaken an activity that swelled my right calf to the size of an American football, I was now a man capable of doing something that no one else had ever done. And the only reason I did it, was because I *did* it.

Everything changed after that. I wrote my first book in exchange for a £4000 advance. I learned to trust my gut and follow my heart and even though I didn't have a bloody clue what I was meant to be doing with my life I felt like I'd only truly get to know myself by experiencing new things.

Now and then I fell back into the trap; choosing to live somewhere expensive, somewhere I couldn't afford by just the few pennies I earned on book sales and speaking engagements. I regressed to doing things I didn't enjoy just so I could pay the rent, then always *just* before it became too late to pull myself back from the slump in motivation that comes when you deprive yourself of the things you need in order to have the things you want, I wrestled myself away from convention.

Slowly I fashioned a career based on adventure, making a living through the stories generated by an ever-growing collection of journeys and projects. But for many years I felt uncomfortable with the *Adventurer* job title. I wanted to earn it, to actually make a living from adventure before I could feel pride at having established my identity. The idea of having my name with a Dot Com after it was deplorable, even three years after I skated Australia. I could self-promote shamelessly when I was able to be completely honest with myself about how I survived. By mid 2010 my values had shaped themselves around the contended realisation best made clear when waking up far from urbania, in a tent or hammock or bivvy bag beside a river or the ocean, rising from a night's sleep completely open to the atmosphere with all the belongings one needs to survive in a bag less than the size of an average torso. No TV, no commitments, no debt: a life completely, absolutely, one hundred per cent filled with things you love to do.

There are compromises, of course, but I see it simply. I had made changes by necessity to experience a different side of life; reducing my overheads to the extent where I had no home or stable base, no permanent partner, no creature comforts, no familiar social circle, no idea when the next money would come in. And yes it can be unnerving – uneasy, even - but less so as time goes on because on the other side of the fence if I had a house and a job I would be compromising my freedom, my love for flexibility and my ability to say yes to the most ridiculous ideas in the world; thus creating a living from my joy because I had time to do so. Put these alternate worlds side by side and there is no real choice for me. I have recognised my abilities and talents, accepted my flaws and failures, understood the origin of my passions and worked hard towards moulding them into a way I can survive in this world. Every single one of us is different but of one thing I am sure; we should all love our work. Each of us is able to create an existence unique to our individual self which enables the answer to 'what do you do for work?' exist as something along the lines of, 'I do what I love, and I couldn't imagine doing anything else with my time.'

By early 2012 I had finally broken down many of the conventions that had been taught to me as a child and was living life hard, defiantly, and with a smile. It is always better to accept oneself as the sum of all your experiences and then look forward, only drawing on the past when asked or required. To avoid both a lifetime of being identified as 'The man who skateboarded across Australia' and the aimless drifting that plagued the months following that journey, I created a long-term goal to give me focus. The project was called Expedition1000: a series of 25 journeys of 1,000 miles in distance or more, each involving a different form of non-motorised transport. This was my Yes List (you might know it as a bucket list, but I can't stand the implication that death should be the main motivator behind taking a grasp on life) and my career framework. In between the journeys I would write and speak and plan and perhaps take on a smaller project, and then another expedition of 1,000 miles or more would open up more days, add one more tick to the list, perhaps warrant another book. And so on.

The key behind making a passion project work is to vocalise it, so since the middle of 2010 I had been talking about Expedition1000 endlessly. It featured on my website, it was there, loud and clear, no backing out. But by making it public I had found others to share it with, who could help me learn how to, say, paraglide (not easy when you have vertigo) or Aquaskip (best you go to Google for this one). Following the skateboard traverse of Australia my second big expedition was in a kayak down the Murray River, also in Australia. Then an Australian man named Sebastian Terry, who himself was forming his life around a bucket list called *100 Things*, read my book about skateboarding and got in touch. Within months we had shared a few little adventures and had created a speaking tour around Australia together, which prompted an offer from one company, which led us to pedalling a tandem bike from Vancouver to Vegas in the spring of 2011. That was the third journey of Expedition1000, quickly followed up by the fourth, a Source to Sea descent of the Mississippi River by Stand Up Paddleboard, which at 2404 miles found its way into the Guinness Book of Records for the longest distance travelled by SUP. As a bonus, 82 days' exposure to the sun helped me take another step towards a personal milestone: to become the world's most tanned strawberry blonde adventurer, although this record may not be official.

My time on the Mississippi provided timely consolidation for years of personal and professional development and as I paddled out of the final delta channel in southern Louisiana and into the Gulf of Mexico, the expanded horizons in my line of sight became more than literal. Right, world, what's next?

Two months of post expedition depression, that's what. Frankly, returning to an ever-gloomy England in winter was always going to be a bummer. But it passed soon enough and as with all turns of the year, I found a spring in my step. Of course, there was a girl involved, but I'll tell you about her later.

A few stops on the Docklands Light Railway east of central London there is an endless block of a conference centre named Excel, and in the middle of January each year hundreds of travel, recreation and sport-related exhibitors attract tens of thousands of miserable, pale Britons just in time to catch the last drips of enthusiasm before everyone forgets about their New Year Resolutions. The London Outdoors, Bike and Boat Shows combine in a wondrous display of hope, in a building that could house several football fields, at a time of year when everyone in the country has forgotten what sun looks like. Utter genius. I'd been invited to be one of eight competitors in a multi-day Stand Up Paddleboard Racing competition to be held in an enormous Watersports pool at the end of Excel, which would have been fine if the other seven competitors weren't seasoned athletes and my nature didn't involve things that take a long time, very, very slowly. I have the twitch fibres of a tortoise without legs, and didn't fancy my chances.

The product of spending countless months in your own

company is that you know yourself very well indeed, so I wasn't surprised when I achieved the 8th spot out of 8 in the first race. And the second. And the third. In fact, there were only two events where I didn't place last, both occasions involved an opponent falling off the board; one was his own fault because he was getting cocky, the other time I offered a little assistance with a solid push. It seemed fair at the time.

The Show also offered the opportunity to catch up with a few friends and sponsors who had shown me support at some point in the recent years, and I also dedicated a bit of time to folk who were planning a new adventure or hoped for some advice on how to get started with one. One of these was a chap named Paul Everitt, an adventurer who operated under the brand Going Solo. He was from Up North but I tried to look past that, he was planning on building a raft all Huck Finn style and float down the Mississippi, an adventure so effortlessly cool I experienced a rare wave of envy. I offered some thoughts on the river I now knew so well and the conversation then turned to what I had on my agenda. 'I'm open to anything.' There was a glint in Paul's eye, the look of a man who has accepted opportunities and relished sharing them too.

'I have a Bikecar,' he said, 'would you like to take it one thousand miles?'

'Yes,' I replied without needing a second. Then we shook hands.

See, you open yourself up to chance and suddenly luck knows where you live, even if you don't have a house.

3

Sail Away With Me

The slump that chased my Mississippi paddle forced me to assess the dividing line between happiness and sadness, a chasm I have criss-crossed countless times since I decided to try and create a life with limitless boundaries. I'm not ashamed to say I fall helplessly and feather-like into lowness following most expeditions: recalculation and indeterminably slight depression claim my creativity, motivation and joy, despite unacceptable (but necessary) amounts of caffeine being poured into my system. It used to bother me but now I accept these post-journey grumps as part of the process and like any break up all you can do is be positive and let time apply the medicine.

These blues are both unsurprising and a worthy price to pay for the healthy, happy days of an expedition so full of challenge, vibrancy and newness. Only by refining how you judge beauty can you find contentment in black and white pictures after experiencing a full range of colour. Just as I lessen the bravery of my decision-making by viewing the possibility of failure as a positive, I embrace my depressive self wholeheartedly; partly because it's cathartic, partly because nobody else will. Besides, contemplation is a dish best served when staring at one's own navel.

Had I remained behind a desk with my back to a third-floor wall - a cubicle mentality caressing the ambition-killing comfort that routine, regular paycheque and screensaver-with-exotic-beachscape served me daily - I wouldn't know myself in the slightest. We westerners live in an age where the weak can survive for eight decades and where survival without trying is now a right. The gift of being born into fortune is often repaid by squandering endless opportunities, turning a blind eye to our dreams because they're not sensible, and the acceptance of an innate fear and discouragement of peeking beyond the very lip of the box into which we were delivered. We rarely do ourselves justice. Innovators and creators are labelled as crazy. Such is the ease of modern day life we become ruthlessly fond of blaming others for everything that goes wrong in our lives, often without twitching a muscle in self help.

It pisses me off.

But that's just because I was lucky enough to be caught

slap bang in a turbulent confluence of ennui and despair, stale love, soul-destroying work and passionless personality. By the time I turned 25 my best story was that I'd been given two chickens for my 21st birthday and named them Tikka and Korma, there was no denying that I'd become a feckless loser. Once at rock bottom there was little more to lose, so I made something of myself. You lift one finger to the world with enough feeling and the rest of your body follows, and before you know it you're setting up your own genius business or standing on a stage with a microphone or watching the general public file past paintings in *your* own exhibition, or you're paddling a river, climbing a mountain, writing a book, waking up smiling.

We're all brilliant if we allow ourselves to be. But we can't create that shiny Best-In-Show version of ourselves unless we think and scrape and understand and enable our strengths and act on that unique combination of what we enjoy and *who* we are.

Had I remained behind that desk I wouldn't have battled hypothermia in the Snowy Mountains, wading for days through thigh-deep snow just inches from a deathly drop-off, having expected nothing but a summer's walk. I wouldn't have taken the plunge and chased a girl overseas just to experience two weeks of shattering confusion and heartache in Mumbai. I'd never have believed I could recover from tipping my kayak in fast-moving water, then guide my fast-submerging craft to shore whilst retaining the attitude to address the waiting 6 foot Brown snake with an angry, 'Piss off! I've got enough to deal with without you!' I know every layer of myself and how I react when I'm almost dead, starving, in sheer emotional despair, suffering from immoveable fatigue, in grave danger, folded in physical agony, sensing faint hope, drawing on grit, in the midst of change, waking without knowing the whereabouts of my next bed, making 99% of an audience laugh (there's always one person sleeping), experiencing happiness, thrill, joy, exultation. I know my equilibrium, I'm familiar with my lowest ebbs and I know I'll never quite reach the top rung, but I'm content to continue climbing. I know myself inside and out and as a consequence, when something is up, I recognise it instantly and just as fast conclude to seek out a reason, then a solution to level my ground once more.

Which is what I was up to in late 2011, hair still singed blonde from the Middle America sun, white eyebrows mercifully losing their distinction as my skin slowly faded back to its natural translucence. I was lost. Straight off the back of my favourite journey that had ticked every single box I now faced the opposing side of my reality. Home time. The in between expedition Dave. The Bruce Wayne to my Batman, the Peter Parker to my Spiderman, the Clark Kent to my Superman. There were two opposing halves to a puzzle that didn't fit together and I needed an answer to cement the gaps. I was footloose and lacked stability. Two obvious factors were missing from the conventional side of my brain: a place to call my own and a partner to love. With one or both of these, I figured, I'd lessen uncertainty, increase independence and gain a consistency that would bridge my two worlds. Immediately I ignored the only one true lesson I'd learned during my dating days and set about *actively* seeking a partner. Stoopid. I really do have a habit of compromising myself by getting excited.

Predictably, I fell hard for an utterly gorgeous (tick) Paediatric Doctor (tick) who had once gone on an adventure (TICK) and seemed conflicted over whether pursuing her medical career would get in the way of what she really wanted to do, which I read as: *please take me on adventures forever*. Naturally I became excited about all the possibilities, ignored the fast-gathering red flags then failed to listen to the reasonable side of my brain, mainly because my heart was beating too loudly.

It's happened before. Career girl realises that the very wild and brave and kind and rugged qualities that she's attracted to also indicate antipodal life choices. Then she tries briefly to change the boy by questioning his life purpose and wondering out loud whether he can honestly consider himself a valuable adult by making a living from adventure. Eventually, upon realising that these two lives cannot fit together without drastic change, girl seeks Mother's opinion and becomes child again when Mother responds with: 'Everything this man stands for goes against everything you've worked towards.'

In fact, throughout the whole period (which lasted about fifteen days but felt like seventeen years) I was forced to actually contemplate whether I had made the right choices in my life. Who am I? Do I really want to live like this? Can I justify never being able to have a relationship with a Doctor just because I like waking up in a tent some of the time?

I concluded, but not until she had stood me up for the fourth time in a week, that it was a desperately needed wake-up call; I needed a woman who understood me because we actually shared the same values, not just because she *wanted* to. And most importantly, I should never go looking for love with a picture of what it should look like in my mind, because you can't shoehorn a human being into a perfect relationship, however perfect her little face is.

So, with finding a woman temporarily erased from my task list, I set about looking for a flat to rent.

*   *   *

'Are you sure finding a place is so important?' Emily asked, 'I think if you have the right person in your life then you have a home wherever you are.'

'That's all very well,' I said, 'but where does one find such a person?'

One week before things came to a head with the Doctor I found myself on a train with another girl. We were squeezed in next to each other on the 19:30 First Great Western train from London to Plymouth, Emily heading to her parent's house, me to a short-term work project. Outside, the last of the days' light had departed and the fuzzy fluorescence of the Capital slowly filtered to nothing. The two of us were left to get to know each other over a picnic dinner that Emily had accumulated from a supermarket in Paddington Station. It was a marvellously perfect selection considering she'd never fed me before.

I wasn't dressed as me. The last time I'd worn a suit was sometime in the late 80's but the previous day I'd been filed in as a last-minute replacement motivational speaker for some IT company, agreed to break my week in the south-west, bought a suit and made a day trip to London in return for a healthy sum of money. I earn enough from speaking engagements to survive, but this was the one and only gig ever organised for me by a speaking agency. I was beginning to recognise that the corporate world only tended to consider adventurous speakers if they conducted miserable expeditions with endless examples of near-death experiences. Sadly, if I actually had a financial advisor they would be left disappointed by my careless (and not always successful) pursuit of amusement while on a journey; which remains fine by me, because corporate speaking gigs are often near-death experiences in themselves.

All that said and done, the choice to jump on an early morning train in order to pretend that I had a grasp on teamwork motivation proved to be worth it purely because of the ride home. I just didn't grasp the gravity of my company at the time because my head was still focused on the pretty Doctor.

A few days earlier, in mid November, Emily and I had

met at the Royal Geographical Society's *Explore* weekend that brought together explorers, adventurers and anyone else who wanted a taste of the good stuff. We found ourselves sitting opposite each other with lunch on laps in small cardboard boxes. I recovered remarkably quickly from that first glance into her big blue eyes and teased her for choosing the vegetarian option at exactly the same time as hypocritically ruing my bowl of meat, which shared the consistency of plastic. Between us sat Alastair Humphreys, his bearded face strongly contrasting with a newly shaven head. Had we been strangers meeting in a dark alleyway I would have feared for my life but Al is a one-off, a rare breed of trailblazer who refuses to blow his own trumpet despite a ridiculous list of personal achievements. In the eclectic world of non-TV Adventure he stands alone at the head of his field; communicating, sharing, enabling others through writing and speaking and walking the talk. But on this occasion Al didn't exist. He knew his place and slipped away unnoticed, leaving me to refill his seat and shuffle just a few inches closer to Emily Penn, who just happened to be the only person I'd ever met who made me feel lazy.

*   *   *

'Have you ever swum with Humpbacks?' In seconds Emily had a laptop on her knee and a video playing, the unmistakable song of whales resonating through the train carriage. She educated me on issues from ocean plastics to overfishing, regaled tales of speeding around the world on a record-breaking Biodiesel-powered spaceship-slash-boat named Earthrace, to spending six months in Tonga where she organised the largest ever single-day rubbish clean-up operation. She had hitchhiked onto cargo ships and crossed the Pacific, gotten lucky in Vegas and rode a train from England to China because flying didn't seem like a suitable way to travel. She was a Cambridge Architecture graduate and an unqualified mixture of English and Welsh but was now based in America guiding the formative stages of a business named Pangaea, which involved a 72ft yacht and lots of scientific exploration in the high seas. It's fair to say that I recognised my own insignificance that evening, at the same time as sensing the early stages of a great friendship. Across the aisle we were both aware of other travellers staring open-eyed, giggling amongst themselves at the bizarreness of the discussion *over there*. I suppose it's rare to hear tales of pirates swiftly exchanged with world records and long distance skateboard journeys.

Our legs brushed and guilt swept through me, *what about the other girl?* I was desperately trying not to have bad thoughts, and having yet to realise the imminent disappointment of the Adventurer-Doctor relationship I was keen to retain my physical integrity, at the very least. I had known spending time with Emily was asking for trouble a few days earlier when our post-*Explore* goodbye at Monument Underground station turned into the Greatest Non-Kiss Ever, but despite her lips, her walk, her eyes, her intellect, her hair, her face and that *certain something* that I hadn't managed to pinpoint yet, I was still capable of behaving. Perhaps I was becoming an adult, after all?

*   *   *

Adult? Maybe. Hopeless romantic and skeleton key to any door standing between the present and potential butterflies? Always. Perhaps not so secretly, I was instinctively drawn to this girl. I had no idea how she had evaded my radar until now; where the hell had she been hiding? Emily had no play whatsoever on my flitting relationship status in the days following that train ride, but our friendship developed swiftly over Skype once she had returned to the States. Without being conscious of it, I was on a mission to engineer more time with her. 'I'm looking around for somewhere to go for a couple of weeks over New Year's,' I told her. 'I'm desperate for some sun and writing time.'

'Try Spain,' she offered, but I was having none of it. There were sniffs of interest from a film company in LA who had received an early draft of my new book and thought it had potential as a movie, but although it just seemed like white noise the lure to California became stronger.

'I have a few friends in LA who'd I'd like to catch up with,' I told Emily, 'but if I came over would you spend some time with me?'

'Maybeee,' she cooed.

It's worth being persistent. On Boxing Day 2011, just a month after we had met, I flew to California to be met at the airport by a girl I'd never even kissed before. It was an audacious, mad leap into the unknown, but we leapt together.

She patiently lay on the couch of number 210 ½ just a quick walk from Del Mar beach as I read out loud from the manuscript of my second book, which would be published a few weeks later. I suppose a book about my relationship history and a challenge to date one hundred women in one hundred days was the perfect litmus test for our own relationship. Em's head rested on my lap, unless I reached an uncomfortably candid section or to my shame, a sex bit, in which case she'd squirm away to the far end of the sofa.

We discussed our dreams and visions of a continually peripatetic life. She articulated the reality between controlling the conventional desire for a partner to share this wonderful life with, and the difficulties of truly living in the moment when your soul is intertwined with another. Everything I'd been incapable of unlocking for myself, this girl was unravelling for me. I was still caught between the thought that I needed a partner with the reality that my lifestyle was at its most efficient, less stressful – and, arguably, more enjoyable - when I was single. No wonder relationships became my focus between adventures; it was exactly then that I needed something new to fill my time.

Neither of us were prepared for anything truly serious but regardless, we lived every one of those moments in Del Mar alongside each other without a care in the world. I wrote. She painted. We topped up ceramic mugs with wine and wandered to the beach each night, each time hoping the sunset would put on a show. It never did, a thick layer of dark grey cloud on the horizon soaked up the kaleidoscope of pinks, reds and oranges that we were both so familiar with from our personal ventures. One Day We Will Have a Sunset said the bafflement between our desperate stares. We let the washing pile up by the sink, danced spontaneously beside the eggs in Vons Supermarket then regained our energy with Em's home-baked cookies, endless bars of chocolate infused with nibbed hazelnuts, and little glasses of green superjuice.

We were shamelessly unsociable on New Year's Eve, she introduced me to her friends and it took about three seconds before we started to ignore everybody. The party drifted to its climax, a characterless place which could only be described as an even split between Dixie bar and old people's home. Ordinarily, you'd expect New Year's Eve in California to be a raucous, out-of-control affair, but despite the venue being depressingly downbeat and full of pensioners I was utterly content and couldn't take my eyes off her. I felt like a lost puppy whenever she disappeared into the crowd. The battle back from the loo was excruciating, so many Americans with fading hair and bingo wings blocking the way. We were ready to go before the clock struck midnight; we floated in each other's arms, the craziness of that last-minute swoop into LA making complete and utter sense. God we were rude, but it was glorious.

*   *   *

'Does sailing count towards Expedition1000?' Em asked, peering at me over her laptop. I glanced back,

'Yep, are you going to teach me how?'

'I have an idea.'

It wouldn't be the last time she spoke these four words. Just a few hours later we'd roughed out a plan for the 5th journey of Expedition1000. Emily's role as Pangaea Explorations' Programme Director was all encompassing. Her mission was simple and although I'm paraphrasing a little it was basically: *save the world*. Through Sea Dragon, the company's yacht, Pangaea aimed to open up access to the oceans to scientists, researchers, students, divers, presenters: anyone who would contribute towards shedding more light on the blue part of our planet that protected so many mysteries.

We took the highway south to San Diego, where Sea Dragon was moored in a marina on the bay side of Point Loma. Em had a few odd jobs to perform but wanted to show me around the boat. Sailing is a world I've never been a part of, so I kept thoughts like *that boat is big, that boat is shiny, those ropes look heavy* buried deep inside my brain, at the same time as making my face seem confident and impressive. Em, a former RYA Yachtsmaster of the Year, probably wouldn't take kindly to me not knowing what a mainsail was. We scrambled up a ladder, opened up the hatch and slipped below deck. A wide-open galley and saloon lay ahead, leading to a narrow corridor with two cabins and the heads (toilets) up front. A passageway wrapped in both directions from the bottom of the entrance steps back around the engine room, with twelve bunks stacked in twos and threes towards the stern. Em was in her element, gliding and weaving through this floating Hobbit Hole, and I did my best both to keep up, and reduce, personal damage caused by multiple collisions between my head and the damn boat. Despite the swift dispatching of my comfort zone the moment we had left dry land just being on Sea Dragon gave me a sense of how ocean travel was possible. 'So, when are you taking me to sea?' I asked. She smiled, took my hand, and led me off the boat.

Although Sea Dragon had plotted a course across the Atlantic and back the previous year the plan for 2012 was focused west of the Americas. 'We're running a three-leg research trip to study the spread of debris caused by the tsunami that hit Japan last year,' Em explained, 'but in March we need to get Sea Dragon to the start point in Hawaii, probably from Mexico. Reckon you could find ten people to sail across an ocean?' I raised one eyebrow, and then the other, mainly just to erase the wrinkles in my head so she would forget that I was 8 years older than her.

'Maybe,' I replied.

'I need to fill this passage, just wondering if there's a way we could make this work for you, too,' she said.

'Is it over one thousand miles?'

'It's close to three thousand.'

'Just so I'm getting this right, do you plan on being on board?'

'I'm not sure.'

For some reason, a great amount of enthusiasm for the opportunity to make my first ocean crossing was reduced to absolute zero when I realised she might not be involved.

'I don't know whether I could rally that many people,' I said, 'but either way, I'm not sure I'd be interested unless you were there too.' I was serious. Sailing would take me to a new place geographically, but would lack the physical challenge I'd fallen in love with on previous journeys.

'It's not a very testing trip on its own,' Em thought out loud, glancing at her laptop then back to me, 'there would have to be something new about it for me to justify three weeks at sea.'

'Am I not enough, EP?' I teased.

She ignored me, rolling her eyes.

'What if we tried an experiment?' she said, 'there could be workshops each day about everything from ocean plastics to relationships, happiness to social media. Each day a different crew member could take the stage and share their expertise and passions with everyone.' She was on fire!

'Like a TED conference, at sea?' I added.

'Exactly, we get a bunch of people onto the boat for three weeks away from the pressures of land, then see if there's a change in mindset.'

'Ok, where do we start?'

Within two days Em had roughed out the logistics and I'd written a synopsis for the journey and posted an advertisement for boat positions on my website and social media channels.

'No commitment at this stage, we'll see what happens over the next couple of weeks and make a decision then,' she said, noticing my bristling discomfort at planning something a whole two months in advance. I smiled, thankfully. In truth, I didn't hold out much hope. Each berth required a spare couple of thousand just to make the voyage viable and having never attempted to tap my extended network for commercial possibilities I had no idea what the reaction might be. That said, this pipedream's silver lining was twofold; a new expedition was potentially on the horizon, and Emily Penn appeared to be the female version of me. Just prettier, and with a rocket-powered brain.

*   *   *

All of a sudden, the time came for my return to London. Ironically, just as the lurking pressure of my new flat requested that I was there to justify the outgoing rent, that very base was pulling me away from a woman who had made me feel more at home than anything or anyone in a very long time. Where Em and I went from here though, both personally and professionally, wasn't at all clear. From the moment we had shared our first, ice-breaking kiss in the parking garage at LAX airport, releasing tension, revealing so much and setting up an utterly perfect two weeks, we'd both been open to everything at the same time as holding ourselves back, from everything. Neither of us wanted complication, we lived similar lives in different worlds, had no idea when we'd see each other next and knew that shared moments were the only ones that would further forge our friendship. I cancelled a visit to LA to see other friends; there was nowhere else I'd rather be; yet we were both careful with our words as the goodbye approached. Honest with our mutual contentment but clear about non-commitment, willing each other to continue being free while pledging to stay close. I could only find one way to tell her how I felt without breaking these silent, essential rules. Before driving north to the airport we completed the last batch of washing up, brushed cookie crumbs from the floor, polished off the superjuice and then I folded my arms around her waist and spun her towards me.

We kissed, gently rubbed noses, nuzzling, caring. And then I pulled back a few inches, stared into her eyes and whispered, 'I love you…a little bit.'

4

London

Less than two months had passed since my Virgin plane lifted off from LAX, speeding into the sunset and taking me further and further away from Em by the moment. This was my life now; even while sitting nothing remained constant. So much promise lay ahead, the first months of 2012 were slowly concluding the pregnancy of several ambitions and in the absence of terrible luck there is only one true thing that follows gestation: life.

Two weeks later I was holding the first solid copy of my second book, Date. I'd chosen to turn down three offers from publishing houses in order to self publish this book, which was fashioned from diaries written four years previously. My decision to buck formal publishing wasn't taken lightly, but the privilege of receiving validation from a publisher was outweighed by a need to retain control of my creative copyright. Few sensations have given me more pleasure than the first time I saw my debut paperback, BoardFree, on a bookshelf, but by gladly selling my story to Anova Books in 2007 I had unknowingly given part of myself away. At the time I was blissfully happy with the decision but I was also naïve about my future. Fast-forward five years and I had established my own unique career, completely sustainable without reliance on external factors. There was no guaranteed book deal, no corporate financial sponsor, and on more than one occasion I'd closed discussions about my involvement with television or film projects that could have proved lucrative but would have held me in the same location for up to six months, thus drowning my energy and nature.

It was all exciting stuff, but especially since I'd started spending time in the United States the words 'We could make you famous' always had the effect of putting me off, rather than nurturing much excitement. It was all so superficial. I was earning pittance but with so few outgoings I was having the time of my life, debt free. Each of my projects was independent from the rest and the only consistency was an urge to conjure new stories and challenges out of nothing but the smallest seed. Similar to committing to paying off the huge cost of a house or a car, any choices that would result in my having dependence on others would limit my creative control, then naturally damage my motivation. No amount of money would be worth that, and although of course I remain open to the potential of presenting on TV or signing a J.K Rowling-size book deal, I'll only do it if my life will be improved and my freedom not hindered. I am in no hurry to forego my present by working towards long-term security and hope that my passions can enable me to both enjoy my youth and produce passive income that will last forever. I see my books as my pension, which is a great incentive to write more.

Two prior decisions influenced this train of thought. Firstly, the majority of filming and the entire post-production process of a documentary made about my skateboarding trips had been taken out of my hands. I hated the removal of my input on telling my own story – it felt like invasion - not to mention the diminishment of my enjoyment of those journeys due to the ever-present effort, stress and lack of trust, all factors that sadly flourished amidst the intensity of near two hundred days on the road with a film crew.

Then, despite the joy and professional confirmation of the first book deal, as time went on elements of the book were suffocated. Even now, as I write this in February 2013, the Publisher refuses to make the book available for e-readers, the stock of remaining hard copies are wearing thin, and any attempts I've made to reach a resolution have been ignored. I've never expected special treatment, just fairness, and am totally understanding that the income potential of a book about long-distance skateboarding won't have anyone rubbing their hands at the thought of a bonanza payday. But there's more to life than money, and very soon it's going to be difficult for anyone to get hold of that first story of mine. The advance was wonderful at the time, but right now I'd give it straight back in return for the ownership of my story.

With all this in mind I decided that the success of Date would rest in my own hands. With the help, expertise and enthusiasm of my good friends Kate Denham and Nina Chang I translated my dating diaries into a full manuscript, received critical feedback from a close handful of other friends, edited and redrafted and edited some more, then discovered an independent print house and had the first draft of the manuscript made up in 3D. Next was the concept of a photo shoot for the book cover and promotional matter, which was only made possible with the time and expertise donated by my friend Sean Conway. Not satisfied with being a photographic whizz, Sean was in preparation to attempt a world record for the fastest circumnavigation of the globe by bicycle. His personality, energy and professionalism meant that four hours in an east London studio was all we needed to complete the weirdest and most enjoyable shoot of my life. As a spotty, socially awkward teenager I could only have dreamed of spending a morning surrounded by brilliant, funny women who had agreed to attend based on only the promise of coffee and breakfast rolls. I suppose the dating challenge had taught me one other valuable lesson: if you don't ask, you don't get.

The book flew out in the first month; briefly occupied No. 1 in the Relationships section on Amazon, made at least four people laugh, brought together 100 speed daters on Valentine's Day and raised a few hundred pounds for my favourite charity, CoppaFeel! Most importantly, I now considered myself an actual author. Standing proud holding a different book in each hand I realised that a bit of determination, a few hours spent online studying the ins and outs of what used to be called 'Vanity Publishing', and the support and advice of friends was all I needed to be my own publisher. Nobody could ever take that away.

*   *   *

It wasn't long before I started feeling the itch. It began in the kitchen with shuffling feet waiting for the kettle to boil, mind bouncing from book promotion to my next public speaking gig to unfolding expedition plans then to *where the hell February had disappeared to*. It was a grave reminder of how monotony and memory are mortal enemies. Time is supposed to speed up as we become older but with recollections from almost every day of the past half a decade my watch hand was moving slower than ever, and then *zoom*, a full month spent in one place goes in a blinding flash. If you're one of those people who hates their birthday approaching, try using your time well and not only will the dreaded day hold off for a while, but you won't mind when it does come because you made the last year count.

I am still haunted by the lost years defined by my former career: every day the same. Sinking slowly into my sofa-sized beanbags for another brain cell destroying Playstation marathon, my bed a mattress on the floor, hide and seek with the cat, drunken nights on Wind St, the walk or bike to work, that snack stand at the top end of The Mumbles. Blurry memories from years that literally faded by without offering anything essentially important or formative. *I squandered so much valuable time just existing.* Brief flashbacks populate that era in my mind as though trying to recall my early childhood, but without chronology or development. It's almost as though my brain has tried to remove a part of my life that was grossly wasted, leaving behind a thick residue of loss.

Whichever corner section of my tiny brain is responsible for memory has now become toned and supple due to constant activity. The importance of change, newness and creativity isn't done justice by a saying like 'variety is the spice of life,' rather, the human ability to adapt and mould to new situations and tests is self-perpetuating. Such as living a life of unchangeable routine will blend similar memories into each other like sediment, a consistent attitude toward accepting fresh challenges and creating a habit of saying *yes* will forge a positive second nature hard to break. This is why I consider frequent adventure irreplaceably important; the mental, physical and habitual exercise that comes from doing new things creates the basis for our own regular software update. Without this, your operating system gets slower and slower, less able to function efficiently as time progresses.

Although it felt like the right thing to do in mid December, less than eight weeks in the flat had extracted the need for geographical stability from me. I'd been excited about having my own base; putting books in a case, clothes in a cupboard, pictures on the wall, retrieving my desktop computer and other forgotten bits of stuff from my parent's house. But I was too far gone: it just wasn't working. I'd set my life up purposefully to be flexible so I could accept new opportunities at a moment's notice, and the flat and the stuff meant that I now had one big obstacle (and boxes full of smaller ones) standing between me and the next expedition, which, you might be glad to discover, was a voyage from Mexico to Hawaii on a yacht named Sea Dragon. A couple of posts on Facebook later I'd found someone to sublet the room for three months, freeing up my energy for another bout of new memory creation. I couldn't wait. Time flies when you're having fun, but at least you can remember it happening.

5

To the Sea

We hadn't quite gotten ten, but enough people had signed up for The Sail to make it viable so almost out of nowhere I found myself flying back out to America to take on my fifth expedition of over one thousand miles.

This one was ever so different from anything else I'd attempted before. I wouldn't be relying on my own power or mind or even health, instead I'd be an equal member of a crew dependent on the elements and the craft that supported us. Although Expedition1000 was purposefully wide open to all manner of tests, this was the first time the focus of my journey was on other people. Em and I set about planning our little social experiment, first through Skype and then in London when she visited in late February. Like most teachers, we knew there would be an element of *night-before planning* but seeing as we hadn't done anything like this before, keeping the structure organic was essential.

In many ways, having both been privy to the importance of thinking time far from societal demands, we were already certain of at least part of the crossing's outcome. Three weeks of combining discussion about life as we know it with total separation from the stresses of land, work, daily commute, bills, mobile phones, bosses, Facebook, social expectation, media and even food shopping would undoubtedly shed a new perspective on the lives of everyone on board. I was excited, nervous and intrigued about how The Sail would affect me personally. As much as people fascinate me I am most at peace when alone or in very small groups, and the chances of discovering any escape on board a 72ft yacht seemed slight. I'm always at my most vulnerable when open to impact from others and the potential for 'cabin fever' was terrifying. Leading a mission in a totally alien environment was going to be a bloody tough challenge and I was thankful that I wouldn't be doing it alone. In fact, there's no way I could have done it alone. Em was the orchestrator for much of our cobbled together 'syllabus' and on several levels she was my mentor, too. Her experience at sea and in remote communities meant her understanding of many facets of human mindset was considerably greater than mine. At times I wasn't even sure where I was able to contribute to the conversation but I offered a neck rub now and then, just to show I was useful.

A new word entered my daily vocabulary thanks to Em: *epic!* We'd devised our individual epic lives and combining them added flavours I'd never tasted before. The manner of our approach into Cabo San Lucas, Mexico, where Sea Dragon bobbed patiently in the middle of the harbour, epitomised how something so obscenely different and seemingly extravagant from normal life could become effortlessly possible. First though, I had a bigger plane to catch.

My airliner dumped me in Los Angeles, where I hopped onto a southbound Pacific Surfliner train. Two thirds of the way to San Diego from LA I disembarked at Oceanside, where Em was waiting with her trademark smile and nose freckles. Her hair never survived too long after a morning shower before relapsing into a wavy sunburst that always threatened to dreadlock itself at a moment's notice, but on this occasion something was different. The moment was straight out of a movie; I stepped off the train with my bags, the crowds swelled on the platform then quickly parted into the night and all of a sudden there she was. Her hair was blow-dried. It was a miracle! I've always been greatly articulate in these moments and managed to murmur one word to sum up how I felt about this new-look phenomenon before me, 'Hot!'

Em was unique compared to any other woman I knew. She had a tiny wardrobe consisting of three baggy vest tops and a single pair of black jeans that would last her for the best part of a decade. She tended to ignore conventional attraction techniques like heavy make-up, jewellery and high heels, preferring instead to engage in decent conversation peppered with the most delightful giggles. Still, I wasn't arguing with this new vision, all the work on that hair must have taken her at least half an hour, and all for me!

'You look amazing,' I swooned, dribbling.

'Thank you DC,' she replied, fluttering her eyelashes, 'I was supposed to be doing some filming today but they cancelled at the last minute, took me ages to do this hair.'

'Ah...'

Although she had stayed with me during a recent visit to London we'd failed to completely recapture the sheer bliss of our first days together in Del Mar, but our friendship had strengthened and nothing but taking dreams and making them real lay ahead. Both of our eyes were shining in that Oceanside car park, full of ambition and potential for the month to come.

In early January, during my visit to Em in Del Mar, we'd been introduced to Eddie Kisfaludy, Operations

Manager for Richard Branson's Virgin Oceanic project and co-founder of SciFly, a company dedicated to offering high tech sensor payloads in aerial technology. I may have mixed the words up, but whatever order they come in I still couldn't quite grasp what SciFly did. Let's just say Eddie was an intelligent and superbly interesting guy and we had met for breakfast the very next morning to open up discussions about developing a pedal-powered submarine, with a view to travelling 1,000 miles underwater. All in good time.

Eddie was also a pilot, diver and marine expert who owned his own light aircraft, and this formed the crux of our plan to get to Cabo without having to crush onto a passenger jet. We caught a few hours kip then dashed around a behemoth of an American food store, piled two days worth of supplies into the spare seats of his pickup, then drove to a small airfield with Em and I flat on our backs in the bed of the truck, laughing our heads off at the irony that we were on our way to Mexico, and hiding from detection like Mexicans headed in the opposite direction. Not since my single digit years when Dad had his pilot's licence and flights in a Cessna were more regular than family holidays, had I climbed into an aeroplane smaller than a London bus. Em and I grinned at each other as we hurtled down the runway before rising fast above the earthy, concertina landscape south of San Diego. The Pacific Ocean gleamed in the sunlight to our right and within minutes we had passed into Mexican airspace, looking down in wonder at the border fence that stretched ominously to the east.

One hundred miles south we found Customs to be an easy affair, conducted at the ambitiously named San Felipe International Airport, which consisted of one short runway and a single building with red tiles several miles south of the town. We were on the northern fringes of the Baja peninsula, which is separated from mainland Mexico by the Gulf of California, otherwise known as the Sea of Cortez. Tight clumps of small mountains rose from flat desert plains, completely desolate country just daring humans to test their survival skills. We followed the Gulf's western shoreline south for a few hours before Eddie eventually guided us lower, speeding around headlands with jagged rocks just metres beyond the wingtip, showing little regard to the natural placement of our stomach organs with a rollercoaster manoeuvre up and over a couple of ridges. And suddenly without warning, down below a sandy airstrip appeared as if by magic. 'Buckle up, kids,' Eddie drawled into our headsets, 'welcome to San Francisquito.'

The town had a population of four, if you didn't count

the local military who rushed up in a dark green jeep to, wait for it…take photos with us. It's safe to say that San Francisquito wasn't flourishing quite like its older cousin, but for us, that day, it couldn't have been more perfect. Goodness knows how the local family were able to fulfil our menu order in their ramshackle beach café – it appeared that we were the first tourists to land in several weeks – but lunch was good and simple.

A few hundred metres along the beach the ground rose up from the sea and upon the brow of this hill was a disused house, which wouldn't have been too out of place as a waterfront property back in the United States. Sure, it was dusty and there was no power or water, but it was hard to imagine how much transport, labour and expense has gone into building this now abandoned mini-mansion. We squatted there for the night, just to ensure the work hadn't entirely gone to waste.

As if in a daydream, Em and I walked dirt paths hand in hand for an hour, snapping pictures of cactus silhouettes against the enormous, fiery globe that descended beyond the mountains to the west. We returned to our empty mansion via the beach, plucking brittle floral shells from the sand, each one featuring a remarkably round natural eyelet. Had they not crumbled at the slightest squeeze, our haul would have an almost certain future as necklace pendants. As it was, we made it home just before darkness settled with little more than sand in our pockets, a full moon peeking just above the horizon.

I woke early, Em stirring beside me. Chinks of sunlight rippled against the walls of our bare room, which lay at the southern wing of our accommodation. There were no curtains and our window framed a portion of the sea, which simmered slightly in the morning wind. All of a sudden Em sat bolt upright in bed, she'd seen something, 'DC! There's something out there!' We pulled on layers and dashed down the corridor, through the open plan central foyer and outside onto the house's semi-circular balcony, which offered a perfect 180-degree panorama of the Sea of Cortez. For an hour we traced a pod of whales on their morning commute, softly cooing each time a jet of spray indicated a new breach.

'This is really quite nice, isn't it?' I whispered, squeezing Em's hand. The understatement was intended. We were in Mexico, watching whales over breakfast, the sun rising gloriously out of the waves, our plane parked on an arid sandy runway 3 minutes walk down the hill. And we hadn't even started living yet.

*　　*　　*

From San Francisquito we flew south, following the coast for much of the morning before cutting across the last corner of the Baja Peninsula. The final miles of our journey were low-level, buzzing the beaches north of Cabo, drawing astonished waves from the few people out walking their dogs or dipping toes into the ocean. All of a sudden the stacks and arches guarding Cabo San Lucas' natural harbour were fizzing past our left wing and as we rounded the headland we were reminded that the solitude of sailing across an ocean would have to be earned. First, the jet skis, water skiers, parapenters, early spring-breakers, bars and bright lights of Cabo would raise us up on the ends of our toes. Sea Dragon seemed so small anchored in the harbour below; insignificant alongside goliath cruise liners, quietly awaiting another crew for yet another epic voyage.

6

Cabo

No matter what the journey, the first true step beyond my comfort zone is meeting my transportation. The wonder I felt at unwrapping Elsa, the unique, solid, bright banana yellow rollsrolls carbon Kevlar longboard that I would take across Britain and Australia. Then Nala, my Wilderness Systems kayak, lying in wait in a garage in Albury Wodonga, my new friend Ro Privett gleaming at the joy emerging from every crease in my face as I perused my new craft. Having paddled the Murray, he knew at first hand the treats I had in store. Tinkerbella, the Tandem Bicycle that Seb Terry and I would spend the next fortnight on as we pedalled hard to Vegas. Artemis the Lakeshore River Rover, my paddleboard, a familiar yellow, my Mississippi platform, my home, my office for three months on one of the world's greatest rivers. The collision between a total lack of familiarity with this inanimate object, and the wonder of imagining just what you're going to share together. A gurgling, surging upheaval of the gut. The unknown potential of dreams and fears is about to be proved because of *this* thing you've chosen to travel on.

A taxi had deposited us at the gates of the waterfront complex, an extravagant horseshoe of cafes, bars and stores, each packed to the brim with tourists all around. We reached the dock and Em made a beeline straight for the Sea Dragon dinghy, which was moored to the closest possible pontoon. Two violent tugs of the starter cord and we were off, chugging out of the marina past multi-million dollar yachts and hungry sea lions that almost hovered behind whichever fishing boats were throwing out the most lunch. Although we'd met already in San Diego, at the time there was no journey planned for Sea Dragon and I, so as our dinghy bumped out into the open harbour and rounded the yacht I stared at the naked mast rising 90ft above deck, the slight waves disappearing beneath a sleek hull, the canopy above the wheel to the stern, the intricate web of ropes and wires that would contribute to this next expedition. I was lost. No idea where to start. Hopeful. Vulnerable. But ready.

'Tidy those ropes up.'

It wasn't a question, and considering I'd been on board for all of ten minutes, my bags were yet to find their way to a bunk and Captain Dale was already becoming someone I wanted to avoid as much as possible, the future did not look Orange.

'Here's how you do it.' Jesper, the Danish deck hand for our upcoming passage, had years of experience at sea and his calm, gentle manner provided a natural balance to the man in charge. He skilfully scooped up yards of rope, spooled them around his right hand and then with a quiet, 'like this…' he neatly fastened a knot to hold the loop of rope in place. He skipped up the side of the boat, beckoning me to follow with a jerk of his head, and monkey-like clambered down into the forepeak – a storage room towards the front of the boat - to hang the rope alongside its colourful brothers and sisters.

*   *   *

'So are you together, or not?'

Emily and I looked at each other and back at Dale. We didn't have an answer.

'You either are or you aren't,' he said, 'we can't have confusion like this, it's pretty straightforward.'

Dale Selvam, Captain of Sea Dragon. Although he was a touch over six foot I couldn't quite work out the size of the guy, but with the three of us squeezed down one of the boat's rear passageways we had no choice but to be in each other's faces. The Captain was in his element. Dale relished any chance to spray his turf and my patience, usually thick as a vault door, was already wearing thin after less than two hours in his company.

'However we play things, it'll work out fine,' I said, staring at him.

'I guess we'll see, won't we...' grated his rough, Kiwi accent, glancing first at Emily then back to me, '...this is going to be interesting.'

*   *   *

Em and I hired a car and made our way north-east from Cabo, almost retracing the route we'd made earlier in the week, except now we were two thousand feet lower. We spent the weekend by the Gulf in a little town named Los Barriles with a former Sea Dragon sailor, Sara, and her partner Seth, who had a few adventures under his own belt including a length-of-the-Americas road trip by biodiesel truck. These were the final two days for Em and I to escape before our new family descended on Cabo. We ate, drank, got our jeep stuck in sand, found our rhythm and enjoyed the company of good people, a more relaxed definition of *epic*.

*   *   *

Even on the ever-so-slight wash in the harbour I was aware of the effort it took to stay upright on Sea Dragon's rocking decks. Common sense dictates that time dedicated to a task will always increase familiarity, but I relished the discomfort of being out of my natural environment once again. That heightened awareness of how strange a typically everyday function *felt* was a chance to reassess the things I took for granted, in terms of health, pattern and conscience. Once we made our way out into the ocean the process would change once again, but first I had a few days to find my flat-water legs and becomes used to life not quite on the level.

The team arrived one by one in the days leading up to our departure. All had somehow learned about the voyage through my social media network, but half of them I'd not met personally. Danny Loo had driven behind me for five months as I skateboarded across Oz. Natalia Cohen had invited me to join her table for a pub quiz in Cuzco, Peru. Andrew Cook was a good friend of the Editor of my last book. Tina Beck had attended a talk I'd once given in the UK. Davin Luoma had kayaked a large stretch of the Mississippi River, but although I passed through his hometown of Grand Rapids, Minnesota on my own descent we hadn't actually met before. Nicola Moss was an Englishwoman living and working in Germany. Monisha Varadan was originally from India but owned a business in London. And then there was myself, Em, Jesper and Dale. We gathered together in the open cockpit after everyone had been given a tour, allocated bunks, shown around the galley and fitted with wet weather gear and lifejackets. Most of us were lucky enough to find gifts in our new pockets; leftover treasures from previous crewmembers including jewellery, cash and biscuit crumbs. From my pocket I pulled a woolly hat, the colour of dirty sand, a garment Em grew to be less than fond of.

Dale and Emily, who would be First Mate, held the compulsory safety briefing, leaving us no doubt that we were in the hands of professionals. All in all this would be a fairly simple voyage, a consistent wind was expected from the north east the whole way across, eventually pushing us almost square from behind into Hawaii. The crew was bubbling with excitement; nervous, anticipating something special. I remained quiet much of the time, soaking up lessons from the regulars on board at the same time as piecing together the key moments of that preparatory phase. I still wasn't sure exactly how this journey would compare to my previous ventures but by the time Sea Dragon pulled out of port and motored into open water on a bright, breezy Thursday morning I was exploding with excitement for this new adventure.

Danny and I weren't on board when Sea Dragon left land. Instead, we chugged alongside in a hired tourist boat documenting the departure, the raising of sails, the movement of the crew under direction from Dale. It was an out-of-body experience, lacking the physical attachment to those first stages, but it gave me great pleasure to see Danny leaning over the side, snapping away, his recent new career as a photographer finally doing justice to a natural eye for an image that he'd shown as long as I'd known him. Danny and I first met on a football field in Swansea, South Wales. We played for the same team and he was brought off the bench to join me up front. He had boasted a ridiculous red mohawk, which I feared might pop the ball if he ever got the chance to head it. Luckily, Danny bares resemblance to a Hobbit and I've never seen him head a ball in his life. Not that I can judge, with my own early-twenties shoulder-length mane of hair back then I couldn't hold too much against anyone else's appearance.

We ended up living together and Danny was there throughout BoardFree, taking time off to come and help me skate the length of Britain, seizing the moment once his University relationship failed by committing to the Australia crossing. His dry wit provides the perfect cover for a passive nature, both essential factors contributing to our friendship. He's not afraid to take the piss out of me and his facial expressions don't change when I tell him I have a new, silly project up my sleeve. He's always Danny, whether he's sheltering my skateboarding self from hideous Sydney traffic in late 2006, or taking photos of a yacht in Mexican waters during spring 2012. Always Danny.

Our imminent solitude was delayed by the sighting of a tail. Every boat in the area, Sea Dragon included, became metal shavings inching closer to a magnet. In fact, there were three sperm whales, two adults and a baby, breaching every thirty seconds for ten minutes. The larger flukes were almost as wide as our craft. We maintained our distance, not willing to get caught up in the tourist scramble, enjoying the sight of these beasts in their natural habitat but eager for a chance to be the only boat in view, and perhaps experience our own, personal nature show in the days to come. Finally, Sea Dragon's bow turned west and Mexico became our past; its majestic cliffs slowly turning to a blur, then a sliver, and then, eventually, nothing. By nightfall we were free.

7

Open Water, Open Mind

'You're going on a gin cruise,' suggested a friend, cheekily. Ironic, really, that this friend of mine who just happened to deal exclusively in motorised transport was insinuating that I'd taken an easy expedition option, but maybe he had a point?

I've never had trouble travelling. Forwards or backwards facing on a train, front or rear-seat passenger in a car, sitting high on a stack of bananas in an African truck, the awkward loping of camel trekking in the Sahara – nothing made me sick. Apart from liver. And mango. The blame for this cardinal fruit sin rests at the feet of the Dar Es Salaam fruit vendor who sold me a bag of mango and papaya that just happened to be laced with ants. Hundreds of those little guys in your mouth will make you think twice about the taste again. I've suffered from extreme pneumonia and the odd broken bone, and even the side effects of forcing myself to stay awake for 72 hours on the streets of Melbourne didn't rival the

discomfort that I felt during those first days on Sea
Dragon. For me, the ultimate human endurance feat is to
row across the Pacific Ocean. During climbing season,
more people reach the summit of Everest on a clear day
than have *ever* rowed the Pacific. I don't wish to reduce the
accomplishment of any Everest mountaineer; it is
unquestionably a magnificent feat to scale the highest peak
on our planet, but the sheer solitude, grind, exposure and
mental strength needed to row the Pacific has enthralled
me for years, ever since my first conversations with Sarah
Outen, who became the youngest woman to row any
ocean solo thanks to her Indian Ocean crossing in 2009.
Oots, as I fondly call her, is the perfect example of how to
take on life ambitiously, and with a smile. As Sea Dragon
sailed west Sarah was on the other side in Japan, preparing
for her own Pacific crossing in the rowing boat Gulliver.
Meanwhile, I was experiencing my first taste of being in
the middle of the ocean and my stomach was not at all
happy. I survived for a day before it got me, and then there
was no looking back. Should there ever be a remake of
The Exorcist I'll be right up there at the front of the
audition line, drawing on the experience of vomiting in the
galley sink, in both of the heads (whichever one was
closest – and the fact that they sat opposite each other off
the front companionway should explain the urgency of

seasickness), in a plastic bag by my bunk. What tickles me to this day is that I wasn't even close to being the worst casualty of the rolling ocean. Poor Danny would only recover three days before we reached Hawaii, but at least we'd have a solid reminder of the previous night's dinner after he'd been on deck during night watch.

As the days passed at sea the control freak in me continued to wrestle with the concept of travelling 1,000 miles dependent on the skills and efforts of others, rather than a reliance on my own bloody-minded determination. Suddenly I found myself at the mercy of Sea Dragon's crew, my comfort zone well and truly breached by a *lack* of independence. Functioning as part of a team was not natural for me and I slipped into my cabin every chance I got, terrified that someone would recognise that I wasn't worthy. I had felt something similar in the early stages of my speaking career, when I was caught on stage lost for words, not quite in control of my own reasons or explanations, winging it on pictures of long roads or pretty rivers. I was out of my depth getting paid for telling stories. It seemed too good to be true, too good to last even, and I was always looking over my shoulder ready for the truth to emerge – *I just wasn't good enough.*

I didn't see it at the time, but The Sail was a whetstone to sharpen my character, clarify my personal mission and validate the choices I'd made up until that point. My passion for Expedition1000 was put to the test by poor winds. After three days at sea Dale began regularly suggesting that we turn the engine on and I put my foot down, 'absolutely not.' My utopian image of crossing an ocean under sail had not yet been tempered by the realities of making a commercial sailing trip. This journey was just a means to an end for Dale, he had to skipper us to Hawaii in time for the next voyage, and then the next, and the next, and as a result his sympathies with my personal goals were slight.

Not for the first time I began to see weakness in the ability of my own direct actions to infect others. Thankfully there was clarity through the mist of this disappointment; it was the effort, consistency and lessons of what resulted from my passions that counted. The way my first skateboarding journey fell apart amidst team squabbles was a mystery to me for so long, until I realised that I can't expect anybody to be fully satisfied with my own personal dreams, but me. We all live with our needs and agendas and must flex and compromise when working with others to try and sanction our individual hopes.

After one week and 800 miles under sail power Dale still wasn't happy with our pace and hovered his finger over the ignition once more. He saw my face and didn't press the button, but I retired to my bunk again considering what the 1,000 miles meant to me. Did it really matter? What if we reached Hawaii without a consistent 1,000 miles under sail? Is anyone affected? Am I? I shared my thoughts with the crew and even the sound of my voice talking out loud helped me understand that although one of the reasons for The Sail was to fit into my Expedition1000 plan, that this was just a tiny fleck on the scale of importance for everybody else on board. At the same time, for me it was critical that unless absolutely necessary this journey should feature an unbroken passage of miles, at least into quadruple figures. After that Dale could do what he liked, but we weren't lagging behind schedule by much and I'd be damned if the engines went on prematurely.

Although I hadn't even considered motors being a part of this voyage I understood there was a time limit at stake, but in return for my acceptance of this personal disappointment, I wanted honour for my own aims. I got it, just. After a week of sailing we crossed the 1,000 mile mark and those of us on night watch shared the moment and confirmation of my fifth journey. An hour later, having handed over to the next watch and settled down into my bunk, I felt an unfamiliar rumble from Sea Dragon's bowels. The engines were on, the purity of the trip broken. I dreamed of monsters.

It must have been early morning when Em slipped into the bunk beside me, her warmth bringing life back to my body. The grumbling engine slowly faded into insignificance, my happiness invested in far more than just natural propulsion, sailing and expeditions. I wasn't sure how the rest of the crew felt about the dynamic between Em and I, our initial intention had been to be completely professional but we weren't fooling anyone, not least ourselves. This Sail had naturally formed into a twofold project: our mission with the crew and then our own personal story, of which The Sail was just another chapter. My tendency to latch onto a sole focus in order to complete a long-distance journey wasn't quite as fervent on this occasion; after all, I wasn't being physically tested, unless you count the seasickness. But that said, the moments I shared with Em, whether in the company of the crew, alone on deck or schnuggled together in a bunk, rekindled and then developed the close bond we'd found in Del Mar. I've always thought you should live and travel with a partner to know if you have the potential for longevity, and in addition we were *working* together, fuelling constant creativity in pursuit of the wider aims of this voyage.

Eleven near strangers bound together by a joint

mission. Our vessel became a habitat of developing personalities rebelling against conventional time zones and sensibilities. We lived at a mean angle of 25 degrees, nestled up against the port side of our bunks when not up on deck scanning the horizon for other ships, or gathered in the saloon discussing the necessity for a global change of mindset. Once the crew had overcome the unsettling, debilitating and strangely uniting qualities of seasickness, we grew acquainted with not needing to spend money, operating under no law, our hands free all day from the rigours of clutching, watching and protecting our mobile phones. Five nights seemed like twenty, our small cocoon amidst a vast spread of directionless ocean magnifying our insignificance and shrinking the senseless problems of western living to their true size. Time mattered not. We didn't exist by days, they were replaced by watches; one on, two off. Two six-hour day slots from 6am to noon then noon to 6pm, each of these responsible for preparation of communal meals at their end. Through the night were three separate four-hour watches.

Fast we looked forward to the well-earned rewards of the 2am to 6am graveyard shift, then 12 hours of freedom to sleep, talk and eat!

And all the while, we sailed west. Three ships broke the horizon in the week following our lost sight of land, all cargo freighters. We laughed plenty, although moments of sheer excitement were few and far between, so much so that when from down below Dale threw two items of undisclosed fruit straight up out of the hatch into the ocean, the unexpected splash caused a scramble, and then, subsequently, embarrassment. Our native selves slowly and naturally attempted to break free of land's shackles. Taking the ship's wheel, flushing the loo with a system of pressured handles or cooking on a stove that remained level while the boat swayed around it became as normal as walking to the tube station or checking email. I must admit though, this voyage was not my chance to finally develop any cooking skills. Feeding times were intrinsic to the crew's happiness and having always struggled to cater even for myself I didn't fancy my chances of satisfying 11 adults in one go. Content with chopping and washing up, I hoped my culinary inaction would slip gently beneath everyone's radar, which it didn't, of course. I figured sufficient punishment had already been dished out though, as Emily's pre-trip promises of daily cookies remained empty thanks to a non-functioning oven. Far too late, the cause was discovered to be unforgiveable; the bloody thing hadn't been plugged in.

My life was enriched by a graveyard shift one calm

night. The wind was low, we sighted our first ship for days, then the action began. There had been no marine life since Mexico, our fishing lines trailing lonely off the back of Sea Dragon. It seemed we were sailing over a great, barren, over-fished trench several miles deep, so it was with great surprise that the surface broke around 3am. The cockpit was positioned directly above the majority of the bunks and as the rest of the crew slept we chatted quietly, lifejackets on and safety lines clipped in.

'Did you see that?'

'What was it?'

'There it is again!'

Down below the main lights were off, and there was no pollution to our vision. Still, we had to adjust our eyes to focus clearly on the blackness around the boat to discern whether anything out there was more than just a figment of our imagination, or a navigation light from the boat reflecting back from a wave. All of a sudden there was no doubt that we had company, a whoosh struck through the water to starboard, then another, and another!

We stared open mouthed, not daring to break the spell being cast all around. One, two, five, ten, twenty, they were everywhere, unstoppable, a pod of neon dolphins charging beneath us, jumping, tracing through the water in a burst of phosphorescence. *Wow!* Quickly, quietly, we scuttled out from the cockpit and down the starboard side of the boat, where the majority of the dolphins were congregated. We'd picked up to seven knots, fast compared to our usual pace, but the dolphins' speed was furious and put Sea Dragon to shame. We'd had glimmers of phosphorescence on previous nights as larger waves crept onto deck over the bow, their residue fading like a sunspot on the eye after a mistaken glance up at our star, but this display of nature was a spectacular, unforgettable light show. I worry sometimes that my dromomania means I've become somehow desensitised to natural beauty or even surprise, but witnessing the whizzing, whooshing and bounding of luminescent mammals alongside and beneath the boat in the deep dark of night will always stay with me as a moment of confirmation that knowing so little about our planet is humbling beyond description. It was quite incredible and an eternal pleasure.

Our company remained for half an hour or so but the speed of the dolphins always suggested that their departure could be just as swift as their arrival. After the first minute my mind was on waking Em so she could share this moment, but without a contract with the pod I loathed to wake her in case the ocean once more became empty and dark. Instead, I soaked it up, a shared moment with Andy and Natalia.

I woke up one morning almost on the ceiling. It's not often that happens, but it's also not often that you roll out of bed, stagger down a narrow corridor occasionally slamming into a wall due to the inconsistent angle of the floor, and then pop up the stairs to a totally unrestricted view of ginormous waves. We're floating out here in a small craft upon a ruthless, unforgiving monster. If the movement of the ocean is the monster breathing, it had enjoyed a bit of exercise during those days of heavy swell in the middle of the voyage. We were sent word that a storm was thumping 30 foot waves against the northern Californian coast hundreds of miles off to our right: there was always a good chance that I'd end up back on the ceiling during the next nap.

Welcome to life at No. 1 Ocean Drive, home for now, the only place on the street. Now and then an albatross comes to say hi, swooping in on the wind with a span of near two metres, surfing the swell for a while before disappearing off towards the horizon. Over 1,000 miles from land in every direction, where does an albatross sleep, exactly?

Sailing from Cabo to Honolulu would take Sea Dragon across three separate time zones. One afternoon, completely at our own discretion, we decided to set the clocks back two hours to align ourselves with what would eventually be Honolulu time. We were all happy to enjoy an additional two hours in the afternoon, especially Danny who, when asked whether he had a few moments to lend a hand answered, 'I've got plenty of time! I went to bed for a few hours, then woke up and it's the same time!' The extra hours also led Captain Dale to fidget and create tasks for the crew on watch.

'We need to clean the boat. It's filthy.'

Monisha shut him up with a brief 'No it's not. You're like my Mum!'

We carried on enjoying a lovely afternoon. Again. Without scrubbing the boat.

The horizon, twelve miles away. Our minds have no way to collar down that kind of distance with no permanent perspective, no sight of land or tangible indication of speed. Each momentary 360 degree landscape, all 450 square miles of it, is rugged and ever changing. Larger-than-average waves have been crashing square onto the side of Sea Dragon, drumming the stiffness of water through everything inside. I can sometimes see the sea through the upper port window from my standing position in the galley. Yes, I can see the ocean through the skylight. This is not south London.

Although a completely open sky had been absent the stars were bright each night, as were the planets. Mars, Venus, Saturn and Jupiter all clearly visible, yet another reminder of how small we are, drifting on this planet of ours. Slowly, our lunchtime and 6 o'clock sessions began to form a deeper picture of everyone on board. Each member of the crew has had a chance to share with us their passions and expertise, from photography to firefighting, celestial navigation to plastic pollution and adventure to buying businesses, our time at sea shaped both by the people we were with and our individual abilities to adapt to such a foreign situation in a short space of time. And, I'm strangely glad to reveal, all without a drop of gin in sight.

*　　*　　*

After lunch each day the crew gathered either in the cockpit or slipped around the table in the saloon, with either Emily or myself leading a workshop that we hoped would evolve into discussion to take us though the afternoon. Then, after the evening meal a collection of images taken that day would be narrated by the photographer-on-duty, an often hilarious and original vision of boat life providing a constant reminder that each of us had a unique perspective and way of tackling a task. Nic began to see faces all over Sea Dragon, Davin celebrated St Patrick's Day by taking pictures of green things, Andy spelled out Sea Dragon with parts of the boat shaped like letters. And Danny, official photographer, took just one photo of Nic and Em at the helm in the rain at 6am, then put his camera down for the rest of the day. 'But, the project is called *Photo* of the Day! *One* photo!' he remonstrated when his work ethic was questioned.

The photos were a warm-up for the main event. It was always a pleasure each night when one of the crew took the floor to spend up to thirty minutes sharing their personal story, passion or expertise. We learned so much about each other during these unofficial lectures and the questions and answers that followed. Life stories moulded effortlessly into personal philosophy, each individual on board revealing more about themselves as the days drifted by and we became more comfortable with our company.

While the evening lectures offered a chance for personal sharing, the afternoon workshops were the focus for our voyage game plan. For the first few days, while everyone gained their sea legs, Em focused on exact subjects, like Plastics in Oceans, Acidification, Celestial

Navigation and How a Sail Works. She's a born teacher with a brain capable of networking subjects with even the most distant connection or relevance, but an ability to break down the most complex problems or subjects into layman's terms is one of her greatest strengths. Add to this her trademark ever-moving hands and the odd well-positioned sound effect like a '*whoosh*' or a '*bam bam bam*' and she could teach an Eskimo how to ride a camel from the comfort of a classroom.

The mission we had created was based on simple principles: we truly wanted to challenge the crew. By taking them away from society into an unfamiliar environment, connecting with the moment out of an apparent comfort zone and slowly finding the right frame of mind to take on new ideas away from the hustle and bustle of cities and human life on land. Ultimately, we wanted the voyage to form a change in mindset and a shift in values. We hoped to get right down to individual and group fundamentals, to determine the shared and unique ways of thinking within our tiny, floating cross-section of population. On either side of the ocean upon which we slowly cross are billions of people contributing to a society and economic practices that simply aren't sustainable. Human beings are a plague on the Earth, and the rate at which we consume and destroy cannot continue for much longer before drastic changes will be forced upon us. The side effects of living in modern-day Western society tend to hinder personal happiness, compromise values and create environmental diseases, all things that by our current nature we sweep under the carpet. Regardless of increasing aridity reducing our ability to supply food, rainforests being demolished at unimaginable rates, oceans dredged by nets large enough to contain multiple jet airliners, our increasingly barren Earth is more than large enough to help us hide away the consequences of our actions, that might impact negatively on our conscience.

We protect our cultures without consideration of collateral damage; we disregard our ecological home for the sake of human tradition and our born *right* to accumulate. Our egos are tragically big, and when we talk about saving the *Planet*, we actually mean saving the *Human Race*. Earth will survive long after the last humans are gone but with a limited connection to nature and constant pressure from the environment we've created for ourselves we struggle to comprehend our actions on a personal level, let alone on a global one.

The first week of the voyage had developed friendships and eased everyone into the idea of sharing with each other. Once our workshops started focusing on subjects like Purpose, Values, Relationships, Finding Your Passions and Happiness, things got interesting. Both Em and I were used to opening up the wormhole with a simple question, 'Are You Happy?' In some ways, it could have been a risk doing that in the enclosed environment of a boat, but to the credit of the crew there was never a hint of cabin fever developing. By challenging a person's decisions, beliefs, state of mind, values and choices you force them to reason, justify or question their entire identity. This doesn't always go down well – and it's worth noting that sometimes these queries offer confirmation of identity, rather than the opposite - but everyone on board Sea Dragon harked from a similar culture and what's more, the aims of the journey had been right there on the advertisement that everyone had signed up to. Regardless of how easy or difficult the crew found it to consider the reasons behind their very existence, the very fact that they'd agreed to come on The Sail suggested that they wanted to explore things a little deeper than the fast-paced life back home allowed.

The gift of time to think and consider is irreplaceably precious, but it's a gift that sadly doesn't have much place in our modern world. I believe that the root of each and every problem humans create can be traced back to us as individuals. We are all the same. We were all born without prejudice, without political affiliation, without a God. Before we were able to comprehend the meaning of tradition and rules and heritage there was no system embedded in our minds that would lead us through life's formative steps. As we grow older most of us become part of a life cycle that wasn't natural to our distant ancestors. We begin to inherit certain ideologies from our parents, our peer groups, our leaders and the information and news sources around us, and without the encouragement to seek out what we actually think and feel and believe, it's horribly easy to become stuck in a way of life formed for us by others. We're all animals and any animal that finds itself in a cage begins to pace uncomfortably, either that or we cower in the corner too afraid to move.

I found myself in the trough of one of these almighty ruts in early 2005 and my journey since then has been far greater than a simple endurance adventure. Slowly I figured that everything I was building my adult life around didn't suit me one bit, and if I was to make the most of my time here I'd need to make some drastic changes from the inside out. Ever since realising that despite attaining much of what a Western adult is supposed to have in a successful life I was still capable of being totally and utterly depressed, I've questioned why I believed anything I once thought. I had fallen into the trap of thinking like everyone else seemed to be. Around the world, large swathes of geographically proximate humans believe in the same God, the same rules, the same political ideologies – they share a common reason for their identity. As humans we all have an intricate genetic base that allows us critical thought and the ability to qualify our individual understanding of our world, but we're also individually unique in our capabilities so how can it be that millions of people think, speak and *feel* exactly the same things? I just can't accept that this is natural. This overly common set of beliefs and principles has to be the result of inherited rather than earned thought, as well as life in a society that doesn't encourage individuality. The reasons for this acceptance of someone else's way of life are understandable but when negative impacts on lives – local and afar – and the environment is the consequence of an ingrained way of living it shouldn't be acceptable. It's not as though thousands of people need much skill or instinct to sit end-to-end in traffic jams each morning; cursing each other, checking the watch, fearing being late to work, their engines slowly swallowing up fossil fuels and releasing toxins into the atmosphere. However humans came to be here, was this really our intended purpose?

We're an over-reliant bunch, more and more so in this era of technological advances. Our smart phones appear to be smarter than us, but rather than use technology to our advantage it often makes us lazy and encourages an attitude that has us taking the world around us for granted. Life is easy; the problems that bother us are rarely of note. Without separating from the herd we have no need to develop survival skills or ambition, and every move we make away from the norm is, on the whole, discouraged. At the same time as having more access, capability, knowledge and information to draw on than any generation of humans ever had the fortune to evolve with, we are actually devolving as a species. How can this be?

Our tyrannical focus on a rosier future means we're prone to compromise the present, and when we're unhappy we pepper ourselves with short-term boosts of happiness in the shape of new, shiny things that we could easily do without. Sadly, our focus is so infrequently on living life in the moment, rather we lose the moment in the rat race or the battle to pay off the mortgage. We each have a sense of needing a purpose. Life comes and goes and there doesn't seem to be a wider plan. We are all just ants running around on an enormous playing field: we live and then we die and the only choice that really matters is how we spend our time. We reach the zenith of our lives so fast, yet how many people truly die happy? How many live happy?

These thoughts were discussed over the course of our 17 days at sea. There was opposition to this suggestion that humans had a damaging effect on the planet, and that western society had the potential to negatively influence our lifestyles. Monisha, a natural businesswoman who had founded more than one company, stood against any notion that western economic principles were anything but essential to our standards of living. Davin, a former US naval engineer, didn't see the point in much of what we discussed as he was content earning money however he could in order to enjoy his time with friends, beer in one hand and a gun in the other. 'But I like playing computer games,' he resisted, 'I enjoy it, why should I stop?' It was a more important line than it seemed, in the context of our position on the globe and the subject of our discussions. Davin's opinion was strong and forced other questions back at us. Why should he have ambition or change his lifestyle, when he was happy with his lot?

One of the biggest breakthroughs of the trip came during the Happiness workshop, just two days away from Hawaii. It's such a common, overused term that the initial point of the workshop had a few of the crew with their backs up. Slowly though, by a process of asking everyone to write secretly on a piece of paper the things that make us both happy and unhappy, something twigged. I stared at my own piece of paper, trying to work out how to define such a broad subject with simple examples, and finally jotted the following:

What Makes Me Happy?

- Having the freedom to make my own choices

- Retaining control of my time

- The moment as I'm standing in line waiting to buy a train ticket, when a stranger leaving town who no longer needs their ticket gives me theirs. This, or me passing on my ticket in the other direction, just makes my day.

'But that just takes away money from the people who work to maintain the train system,' argued Davin. 'You get happiness from taking something away from others?'

'I get happiness from the most simple acts of kindness that arrive out of the blue,' I replied, struggling to understand why Davin had made his point. He had brought it up immediately so it wasn't as if he was purposefully playing devil's advocate, this was actually how he viewed life. Every action has an equal and opposite reaction, you can simply choose to accept the positives, or the negatives. Speaking of negatives, the second part of my Happiness challenge waited on the sheet.

What Makes Me Unhappy?

- Doing something I don't enjoy, for the sake of earning money. Therefore, putting money before happiness.

This was all I had. For years I'd struggled against temptation, splitting my adventures with little web design jobs, which sucked my motivation and ate away at my time. I did them just because they paid well. The moment I'd decided to close the door on this simple but soul-destroying back-up plan and use the extra hours towards my passions, I started making the living I'd always wanted for myself. And what's more, my self-respect improved once I'd finally begun to make decisions based on my values, rather than income.

'I've got a thought brewing,' Em whispered in my ear. For a little while she'd been tensing, wriggling next to me, like a chemical reaction was leaving her hopeless against the thoughts emerging from the discussion around her. She dropped below deck for a few minutes and when she returned to fresh air it was with a theory that wrapped up the afternoon session, and most of the theories we'd dealt with on the journey as a whole.

'I think happiness is a natural state for all of us,' she said, 'we can choose to create more happiness by removing or controlling the things that encourage our unhappiness, like expectation, jealousy and always feeling like a victim. We make decisions that add to our stress levels, thus impacting on how we feel. Do that consistently, and I guess we become more unhappy than happy.'

*   *   *

The Sail confirmed the only absolute certainty I've become sure of: that we have to love our work. As typical adults we spend five sevenths of our time working, a huge swathe of our lives that we can't get back. As the clock ticks down on our remaining hours on this planet we tend to be reminded too often how precious time is only when something bad happens: a car crash, a friend dying, the diagnosis of a disease, being made redundant. I'm convinced that it is possible to embrace life without needing a reminder to do so, to discover the inconsequence of money alongside the true value of friendship, love, kindness and honesty. I think being happy without stuff and waking up looking forward to every day just requires a small recalculation of what's important in our lives. A focus on combining our unique abilities with a goal creates purpose in something worth pursuing with gusto.

By the time the rough approach into Oahu had been conquered, as Sea Dragon found calm, turquoise water and motored past surfer-covered waves towards our berth in Kewalo Basin, there was a wonderful contentment among the crew. None of us knew exactly how The Sail had affected us yet but for most on board little seeds had been planted, reminders to trust in ourselves first and foremost. At the beginning of the voyage Monisha had been open about her initial terror of what might happen at sea. Her friends and family couldn't understand why she'd want to put her life at risk by crossing an ocean, but somehow a ringing thought overcame that fear and led to her signing up. Three weeks in the ocean had changed Mon's perception of a lifestyle once so foreign, 'I'm ready to go home,' she said yawning soon after our first dinner back on land. Home, we all realised, was now Sea Dragon.

8

21 Degrees

We stirred beneath the thin duvet simultaneously, perhaps one of us igniting the other telepathically by showing the slightest sign of life. 'Mmmmm' hummed Em, burying her face deep into the space between my shoulder and neck, her right arm folding over my chest, fingers gently cupping my bicep. A faint breeze slipped across the balcony, leaves whispered against the railings, sunlight dappled our faces leaving cow skin patterns of warmth and cool. Down the hill mist slowly lifted, revealing the city of Honolulu for another day. The temperature was a perfect 21 degrees, no goose bumps above the sheets. We lay chatting for an hour before the rest of the house began to move. We were at peace.

She was letting me into her world and introducing me to her friends, *the things real partners do*. Sizzling came from the kitchen, Kahi and Louise from Sustainable Coastlines Hawaii cooking up a storm inside, just months short of their wedding. If there was a ever a pairing to live up to it was them, and as with all couples truly in love the space around them rung with harmony. It was infectious, all this loving. Even the air rippled with hope, although I've often confused this with the smell of bacon and eggs.

We spent a week jumping, playing, splashing in the lagoon near the marina where Sea Dragon rested and recuperated before her next journey. As a huge Hawaiian Green Turtle glided through the waters nearby, Em happily performed her favourite move in the ocean around me, the *Sea Otter*. She flipped and turned, her arms wind milling in not-quite-concentric circles, her smile so at home in blue, clear water. She organised a friend to take me on my first scuba dive and the three of us ventured into what was for me a brand new, underwater world. I briefly held an octopus, astonished at its softness, delighting at its squirting, graceful escape. We pottered in coffee shops sharing leg squeezes and dreams, cooking up ideas for books to write. TV shows to make. Worlds to change.

She was always busy, always shaping new ideas and projects. Unless we were in the water not a minute went by without Em checking her phone, the silence of life at sea instantly broken by the self-perpetuating circular ethic of someone passionate about their work. When you're heading in the right direction each message sent invites several responses. Start the day with a one-page To Do

List and end it with two. Recharged and ready I was the same, although my aims were less critical than Em's. She had a business to run, I was preparing for what I hoped would be two, relatively quiet journeys. Not for media, not for profile, but for the sheer soul of travelling slow, exploring and digging deep to the depths of my physical and creative reserves. Almost as soon as my fifth journey of 1,000 miles or more had ended, the beginning of the sixth was approaching at breakneck speed.

9

The Birth of New Adventures

I left Em in bed on that Honolulu balcony in the black, early hours of the morning. Without wanting to pull her completely out of sleep I held her tight, kissed her head, her nose, her cheeks, her neck. Whispered in her ear those three little words, the first time I'd said them out loud without adding 'a little bit.'

'I love you...'

But she didn't hear me. Her breathing was even, measured and soft as I crept inside and pulled the door closed, thinking, *I'll have to tell her another time.*

Bags packed, I hopped in a cab and headed to the airport, finally able to get on a flight to Memphis.

*   *   *

Just eight months earlier the group had been waiting on the boat ramp. They slowly came into focus as the surge of the Mississippi River offered weight to each of my strokes. I'd been paddling for nearly two months and Memphis, once a mythical dot on a map two-thirds of the way to the Gulf from the river's source in Minnesota, was about to reveal itself in all its true glory.

The Mississippi Telegraph had been throwing up new friends throughout the summer of 2011, news of my journey reaching the lower stretches of the river long before I did. Two dozen people attempt a full descent of the Mississippi River each year but this was the first season that anyone had travelled downstream standing up. I'll admit, I enjoyed the novelty with which my bright yellow paddleboard, Artemis, and I were regarded. Icebreakers in the United States don't come much better than the winning combination of a world record and an English accent. The hard bit was converting the attention into anything more than superficial friendships.

I'd already been joined by countless others en route down Old Man River but this Tennessee welcoming party was special. I'd first taken a call from Jonathan Brown, known as JB, an enterprising big-hearted Hawaiian who had somehow thought my journey to be the key to bonding several different elements of the Memphis outdoors community. It's hard to fasten down dates and times when paddling down a river but I'd given JB my best guess and endeavoured to make it to the meeting place at Shelby Forest, on the left bank descending some twenty miles upstream of Memphis.

The mood was jubilant. An armada of canoes, kayaks and stand up paddleboards lined the boat ramp, paddlers from the Wolf River Conservancy (WRC) and Bluff City Canoe Club waited, beaming with handshakes, congratulations and hugs.

'We've been talking about paddling the length of our local Wolf River next year,' JB chattered excitedly, 'if we make it happen would you be interested in joining us?'

'If I'm able, of course,' I said, grinning widely. The group of 18 paddlers had left the boat ramp less than ten minutes earlier and were now spread out in the Mississippi channel; yellows, greens and reds, sitting, standing and chatting away, buzzing with the success of collaboration. I could hardly believe it; groups like this are so rare on a journey, and already I was being invited back to join another adventure. Regardless of the fact that I had no idea of my post-Mississippi schedule or that I'd never heard of the Wolf River before, a seed had been sown.

One of the aims of my Mississippi paddle was to

connect riverside communities through adventure and this welcoming crew from Memphis was to be one of the most heart-warming occasions of an 82 day trip. More than any group of strangers I've met throughout a near-decade of expeditions, the assembly on that boat ramp would become a part of my life long after I paddled out of Memphis on a stormy August 2011 morning; dressed, shamefully, as Elvis Presley.

*   *   *

Back to 2012, my sadness at saying goodbye to Em had been balanced by pure excitement for what lay ahead. The final two weeks before I'd left the UK bound for Cabo San Lucas had fastened together a bundle of loose ends. My friends in Memphis had gone ahead with plans for a first-descent of the Wolf River and as soon as it became clear that I'd be back on dry land in time to make it back to the central US, I wrote to them with a triumphant 'Yes! Count me in!'

10

The Wolf

The metropolitan area of Memphis, Tennessee is replenished by one of the cleanest natural sources of water in the world. As the Wolf River flows its 105-mile length from a rugged source at Bakers Pond, Mississippi, it passes through a series of wetlands, which filter water into the Memphis Sands Aquifer through centuries worth of sedimentary layers. Land throughout the floodplain is protected by the Wolf River Conservancy with the aim of preserving natural habitats and connecting people to the river through education and recreation.

I've had the privilege of seeing the efforts of non-profit organisations around the world take ownership and responsibility of their local resources, but I've not yet come across such spirit as the one that surrounds the Wolf River Conservancy. I'm convinced that if every major city in the United States boasted a similar model to the WRC it would reap the benefits of a more rounded community, the benefits of integration between recreation and the natural environment providing priceless opportunities for awareness and self-development.

A paddling journey down the length of the Wolf was seen to be an ideal way to bring further attention to the river and the work of the Conservancy guarding it, but the essential efforts of another local organisation were chosen to be the recipient of any charitable donations raised by the weeklong expedition. Operation Broken Silence (OBS) provide support to victims of child sex trafficking, sadly a virulent problem in Memphis. Rachel Sumner, a close friend of JB's and an Aftercare Coordinator with OBS, was smart as a button as well as being just about the sweetest girl you'd ever have the good fortune to meet.

Just one conversation with Rachel left me in no doubt that the OBS anti trafficking department was in good hands, she knew her stuff and rattled off advice and wisdom whether she was just leaving her part time job at Hueys or speeding around Memphis helping me find an Elvis costume. In fact, Rachel has a running joke that she's always been my personal chauffeur, and her understanding character seems to just about cope with the fact that I still don't have a driver's licence.

It should therefore come as no surprise that when I finally landed into Memphis, eager to join the team who had by now been making their way down the Wolf for over two days, Rachel was waiting for me at the airport. We drove for 45 minutes to the house of Richard Sojourner, an ever-smiling and beautifully warm man who had been present for the Mississippi paddle into Memphis the previous year. We fast made plans to head to the Wolf but first a meal and a beer was pressed into my hands, it would have been rude to say no. I sat back and filled myself while Richard discussed the construction of the spacious, well-lit new conservatory, the structure of which surrounded our impromptu lunch; 'it'll be ready in time for a concert in the winter,' he nodded keenly.

This part of the world has produced many of my fondest friends. Perhaps it's the laid back, right-on-the-edge-of-Southern temperament, or the fact that so many of them have a relationship with the water. But what I've always loved about the team of people I affectionately call 'My Memphis Crew' is that they sure aren't lazy. Right from the off they were organised, active and motivated; from paddling to social organisations they're there for each other, true friends and comrades. My endless moving about means it's so rare for me to belong to a close-knit community, but somehow these guys welcomed me in as one of their own. It's no surprise that I keep on coming back.

My flight out of Hawaii had been delayed by three days because of a combination of spring break and overbooked planes, meaning I'd missed the upper section of the expedition. The team already on the river were making their way through empty country and we hadn't been able to make contact for several hours, so we had no gauge on their progress. Still, we stuck to the plan and after a quick run around a superstore to obtain something resembling a sleeping bag for me, we headed to the meeting point where the Wolf flowed beneath the rather unlovely highway 72 bridge. At first glance the river looked typically muddy of this part of the world, and was flowing gently. A quick inspection upstream, however, revealed the true nature of the challenge ahead. I paddled around the first upstream bend, not having to exert too much energy to break the current, and immediately faced an obstacle course of almost biblical proportions. Fallen logs blocked the channel, which in just 50 metres had decreased from twenty metres wide to three. My paddle struck hidden underwater obstacles every stroke, trees and bushes cowered over the stream with no apparent respect for through traffic, sharp former limbs angled from the surface just asking for trouble. *Wow*, I thought, *this is going to be interesting.*

There was a reason that the Wolf River had never been

completely descended in one go before. JB had made an attempt three years previous and his stories of swamps, snakes and tight undergrowth left us in no doubt that the Wolf's upper stretches were not friendly to humans. Although my grounding in Hawaii ensured that I'd missed what would almost certainly be the most miserable three days of the expedition, I struggled to hide the disappointment. I wasn't too fussed about losing the chance to be one of the first group to descend the entire river, I was just eager for a good, solid test of character. Seven months had passed since I finished my Mississippi paddle and I'd barely broken sweat since then, there hadn't even been a good storm in the middle of the Pacific to get my pulse racing. I needed dirt, blood, fun, gritted teeth, a glimpse at the extraordinary and some hammock nights by a camp fire to celebrate an entire day spent in challenge. It was time to live again.

There was no telling how long the others would be so Richard and I discovered a nearby clearing off the bank and began to gather firewood and set up camp. Nightfall approached then passed without any sign of the crew, and just as I'd begun to assume that they'd hole up somewhere upstream, out of the darkness came a whistle, a hoot and the unmistakable sound of water rippling around the bow of a canoe.

The camaraderie of friends welcoming each other in the night far from the presumed safety of solid shelter, the air fresh with adventure and smoke from a just made fire, the promise of sleep well earned and more of the same tomorrow, and the next day, and the next. Huge, tired grins riddled the faces of the dirty, familiar men dragging their craft up the muddy bank. Dale Sanders, the wiry, chilled grey bearded river rat. JB, buoyant from the struggle so far, his five-toed shoes covered in mud that crept up bare legs to flowery board shorts, ever the Hawaiian. Rod Wellington, a bendy Canadian, dreadlocks held back by a filthy rag, his staple choice of headwear. The three of them, along with another few local paddlers who were already making their way back to Memphis by road, were worn from battle with both the bush and each other.

Rod was an experienced adventurer for whom I have the greatest respect. We first came to know of each other in late 2009 when Rod began his own descent of Australia's Murray River the same week that I finished my own trip down that waterway. Our first face-to-face meeting was a year after that, in Vancouver, when Rod spent hours at the bike store that was prepping a tandem bike for that trip to Las Vegas. He then drove to Tennessee a few months later to spend a day on the

Mississippi during my Stand Up Paddle journey, as part of a reconnoiter for his own upcoming full descent of the Missouri Mississippi waterway. His Zero Emissions Expeditions website and blog always made a thoroughly good visit and slowly, through short, intermittent meetings, we were becoming good friends.

With a task at hand like the upper stretch of the Wolf, communication is key. After the smiles of greeting had passed there was a thick mood in camp that first night, it seemed like some critical rules had been ignored. Underprepared individuals had been invited to join on the hardest, most dangerous days of the expedition. Leadership hadn't been established and agendas were mixed. Rod, especially, was seething. In just three days of wading through swamps, dragging Stand Up Paddleboards and canoes through the undergrowth and keeping a constant, watchful eye out for poisonous water moccasins, the pressure of pulling weaker members of the team along had broken team spirit considerably. I felt Rod's pain. He was used to individual challenges and the freedom of a full reign on choice, it's always easier to look after yourself than others and having general safety compromised in a remote situation is enough to take the shine off any venture.

Dale, JB and Rod quietly set about making camp some distance apart from each other and I weighed up the conflict. I certainly wasn't in a position to warrant expedition leadership, that was a position that should always belong to someone going the full distance; but I hoped my experience would offer some consistency to the rest of the journey. After all, now the group was smaller and stronger than it had been. The arguably weaker or more abrasive individuals had gone home, everyone left was more than capable individually. And, of course, it was night time. Everything seems so much better with the morning sun on your face, a bit of rest behind you and the silent thrill of another day of unknown challenges ahead.

With Richard and I on board as new company the five of us made a slow but steady start the next morning. The feeling was that the thick, gnarly swamp was mostly behind us but there was still an expectation of severe struggles up ahead. I crossed my fingers for more than just paddling, and soon enough the wish was granted. And granted. And granted.

Some months previously there had been an attempt to post canoe trail signs along the various streams that wound their way through the forest, but we weren't always lucky enough to find ourselves in a defined channel. Water was everywhere, spread across a floodplain that sprawled far and wide, making navigation less than easy. There is only one thing to do in these situations, follow the flow. At one point we were making our way down a four metre-wide stream when half the flow left the channel and rushed through a narrow gap in bushes off to the left. My instinct was to follow the narrower but stronger rush and Rod felt the same; he smiled grimly when the general consensus opted instead to continue on the main channel. Twenty-five minutes of paddling later, when the flow had completely stopped, we were forced to turn around and return to the junction, before making our way between the bushes. I wasn't fussed, you don't choose to paddle a waterway like this when time is of the essence, but I was also clean and fresh out of the blocks so had the energy to withstand such minor annoyances.

It was part of the adventure, to make mistakes and slowly trust the growing bond between our instincts and the habitat through which we were paddling. I was full of natural trepidation that first day, filled with joy at a return to river travel whilst standing up on a large paddleboard – one of my favourite experiences in life.

I've always had a healthy respect for water and even holding a Guinness World Record for the longest journey ever travelled on a SUP didn't qualify me for complacency.

I paddled slow and cautiously, and during those hours when the streams split into endless deltas and we were all forced to wade and walk, every step was made with potential danger in mind.

Cottonmouth snakes have little patience at the best of times, let alone during the colder months of the year, so they were always on our minds. Probably a greater health risk, though, were underlying branches and cypress knees, a bizarrely gorgeous trait of nature thought to boost structure and oxygenation for cypress trees. We were surrounded by cypresses almost every day but the knees, one to two foot tall stumps that emerged vertically from tree roots and lingered their domes just above the water's surface, were always looking to knock, upturn or even instantly halt the progress of our boards. Falling from standing onto a cypress knee was not going to do our health any good whatsoever, whether the offending wood was convex or jagged.

Throughout a full descent of the Mississippi River, a crossing of Lake Geneva or a traverse of England, a skill I'd not been required to master on a Stand Up Paddle expedition was how to mount and hop over a beaver dam or fallen log, without falling off and making a fool of myself. Only possible with smaller obstacles half-submerged, I watched closely as Rod and JB showed their already-honed skills, charging full pelt at a log before skipping quickly backwards along their board, thus lifting the nose up and over at the blockage in question. All the while a paddle was used for both balance and thrust, then a quick dash up to the front of the board was necessary to shuffle the board forwards, over and off the log. Considering there were beaver dams every twenty minutes and sections of the river that involved up to ten such logs in as many metres, this trip was going to take some time unless I could negotiate each one without a dunking. Still giggling from JB's most recent failed effort, during which he ended up rolling backwards on his board with his legs wrapped over his head and toes dipped in the water, I took the best part of five minutes to nervously slide over my first barrage and escaped with only bruised knees as a memory.

Those five days spent on the Wolf were a pleasure. Returning to the harmony of travel on water, wide open to the surroundings and fully earning each night's sleep reminded me of the importance of simple living. The Sail had been a remarkable, formative experience but travelling with such a large group in an enclosed space hadn't always been to my liking. In fact, deep down I hoped that sometime in the future Em and I would go back to sea together, just the two of us on a smaller boat with nothing but the journey to enjoy.

Although the core crew on the Wolf swelled each day by a couple of section paddlers, we were spread out enough along our river to avoid any magnification of the squabbles that had plagued the first three days. There were remnants throughout the trip, but they dissipated slowly. Rod made the choice to paddle at the back of the pack most days and he just didn't seem happy. The only thing more infectious than happiness is sadness and this concerned me, because we were due to be spending the first days of the Bikecar trip together and all I wanted was a blitz of fresh air and total freedom, especially now the Wolf had reawakened my taste for adventure.

I was looking forward to spending some time with Rod but also knew that he, like I, was a born solo traveller and was most at ease with his own company. I simply remained thankful for my flight delays excusing me from whatever had gone on up top and instead, I was free to relax, revelling in another day of pulling my paddleboard up and over logs, across shallow floodplains, and through incredible forests like the haunting Ghost River section.

Coyotes screamed through the night. Spread out across a long, narrow sandbar a colourful mixture of tents and hammocks guarded silent, sleeping characters. A low orange glow rested in the embers of our 'one match' campfire and the Wolf River crept past, licking unsuccessfully at the boards and canoes pulled just out of reach. I swung in the Sky Tent, my favourite hammock surrounded by rainfly above and mosquito net all around. It was my private space, a cocoon offering protection from the outside world. Em had been on my mind all week, since our goodbye on the balcony. She flitted in and out when calm, peaceful sections of the river had required little concentration, but each night she was a constant presence. It terrified me, having become so close to someone but still not knowing whether I belonged to her, or her to me. My lifestyle and career choices were always at the point of questions from others, '*how can you have a relationship when you live that way?*' My answer had always been firm, but hopeful, '*when the right person comes along…*'

Emily Penn was the first girl I'd ever met who truly understood my choices and my way of life, because she lived the same way. Despite continents and oceans dividing us we'd simply made time to see each other when we could, not letting much get in the way of our blossoming courtship except for the innate, cautious self-protection that develops when you live life by heart. When that wall is down, you're left with either everything, or nothing. My wall was coming down, there was no question about that, and although I was riddled with trepidation there was also no choice in the matter at all. My greatest adventure would always be love; I'd known that for a long time and had always struggled to build natural blocks of protection. My heart was a jackhammer; nothing would get in the way of my passions regardless of the potential of hurt.

At some point the largely selfish existence that I'd forged for myself would request compromise if something - *someone* - more important came along. Em was the first woman I'd met for years who not only confirmed that I was still capable of loving someone more than myself, but that the world would be a better place when shared. My nature cannot let opportunities pass without exploring their potential; no money or time or price of failure is worth lingering regret and thoughts of what might have been, and I have been endlessly wounded in pursuit of love as a consequence, but I don't regret that one bit. I'll always stand up and fight another day just as passionate as before, no woman can leave a scar in the same place as another and I have plenty of space for more.

But this time, with this girl, there was something different. This wasn't just heart, this was soul, and it was keeping me awake at night.

11

Waiting for the Bikecar

As we rounded the final bend on the Wolf, finally glimpsing my old friend the Mississippi, which lured the final drops from the Wolf onwards to a new journey, the numbers on the water swelled to twenty.

Crowds waited high above the river on the north end of Mud Island as our mass of colour paddled the final metres then scrambled and hauled up the bank. Dale, JB and Rod had become the first people to paddle the full length of the Wolf River in one continuous section, with JB and Rod claiming the first descents by Stand Up Paddleboard. They, along with everyone from Operation Broken Silence and the Wolf River Conservancy, had contributed to a little piece of local history.

I felt nothing but pride for great people with whom I was proud to be friends, and made a silent, honest thanks to the Big River that had brought me into these people's lives a few months earlier.

*   *   *

Once I'd confirmed that I could join the Wolf River expedition, I had started to wonder what to do once that little paddle ended. I had at least 6 weeks to play with before a clump of speaking engagements in June would require me to fly back to the UK. Although my conscience was nagging me to spend that time working on new books I couldn't shake a stronger urge.

'Her name is Priscilla,' Paul Everitt had told me, 'and she's resting in a shed in Eugene, Oregon.'

The Bikecar. The Bikecar! What can I do with the Bikecar? Taking this four-wheeled creature a great distance was a unique opportunity that could slot perfectly into Expedition1000, but only if I made it fit. I thought back to my only previous pedalling experience, the tandem ride from Vancouver to Vegas. Part of the joy of that journey was the ease of a good challenge. Sit, pedal, travel, long roads, stop, drink, eat, sit, pedal, travel... But there was an element of fun to it, too. Seb and I had larked around when we weren't burning our lungs in pursuit of 100 miles each day, making tongue-in-cheek videos and revelling in the utter simplicity of life on the road. I wanted more of that, a reminder that by allowing myself a new perspective by which to see the world the world itself would naturally become richer.

I longed for the openness of solo travel again, the

chance and time to think and be creative just because I could be. I could plonk on my butt for six weeks or trust my gut and make another adventure happen. It was a simple choice driven by two ultimate factors: if I didn't take advantage of the Bikecar now it might never happen, and for no reason other than my own amusement I would create a new pattern, any pedalling journeys should from hereon take place between two places beginning with the same letter. I don't think adventures need to be more complicated than that. Reduce the chance of regret, and make it fun. Simple.

If the Bikecar could be shipped to Memphis I would start there, that was now clear. All I needed to do was find another village, town or city beginning with M. I cast my eyes over a map. Montreal? Minneapolis? Mexico City? Manhattan? None felt right; too far, too near, too familiar, too busy. Instead, instinctively I opened up *Navigation* on Google Maps and typed in Emily's new base, the home of Pangaea Explorations. Miami, Florida. The distance between the two burst out at me like a neon sign: *1,001 miles*. And right there was the only encouragement I needed to start spinning the wheels on the 6th journey of Expedition1000.

Memphis to Miami, on a Bikecar. It has a ring to it, don't you think?

*　　*　　*

With the voyage on Sea Dragon meaning I was unable to organise the shipping of Priscilla the Bikecar to Memphis from Oregon, Rod had taken over the logistics. He was busy enough with his own projects but wanted to spend time on the ride with me, and without his help the god awful task of organising the shipping of such a random vehicle would possibly have cancelled the project entirely.

All that said, the Bikecar hadn't arrived during our week on the Wolf and worse than that, there had been no contact from the transportation company responsible for bringing my new wheels over from Eugene, Oregon. We had no idea where it was, when it would arrive or, as the days went on, even *if* it would make it to Memphis.

The whole shipping process had been unnecessarily stressful for Rod. An original quote for around $400 had somehow risen to well over $1,000 by the time I'd made ground and returned to cell signal in Hawaii, a figure which on its own exceeded the total budget I'd factored in for a month of pedalling. Rod and I then made a deal where I'd help him with cover design for his upcoming book, and assist with other odd jobs over time in return for a financial contribution towards the Bikecar shipping.

We holed up at Dale Sanders' magnificent house up in the Bartlett Hills northeast of Memphis, and continued our wait. We enjoyed Dale's company, the old river rat, our Greybeard Adventurer friend who was the perkiest 76 year-old I'd ever met. His wife Meriam's cooking and hospitality was effortlessly maternal, Rod and I would have been forgiven for relinquishing all expedition tasks and bedding in for a lifetime of comfort. The Sanders' has become family.

I was more than familiar with periods of pause or uncertainty, but with absolutely no control over this critical piece of the jigsaw I spent the week after the Wolf River paddle wondering about alternative ways to spend the next month, should the Bikecar not arrive. Perhaps I could take some time to work on another book but something didn't feel right about this. I needed time to digest the past few moments and thinking time comes best on a tough trip. The monotony of an endurance adventure is the closest I've ever come to meditation and I longed for the cathartic side effects of trying desperately not to think about how far I had left to pedal. Plus, I was keen to explore the American South, a part of the world that had always fascinated me. I mean, how the heck can so many people live on nothing but fried chicken, pulled pork and waffles? I needed to find the answer and this was the time for it.

But the wait continued. I caught up with friends, one of whom, Boyd Wade, took me out to his country property via a brief stop at the country store in Millington, TN, which was home to an incredible array of frisbees and an angry rooster named JJ, which hated the colour orange but loved bluegrass music. As JJ strutted around, Boyd informed me that the store had also been the haunt of a young Justin Timberlake, who grew up nearby. Boyd was in fine fettle despite having a lucky escape when falling ten feet from a deer-hunting platform a few weeks earlier.

The next day Rachel Sumner took me to watch my first NBA game and I was amazed at the show put on at the Memphis Grizzlies stadium. Sport in America is pure entertainment; FedEx-sponsored parachutes laden with gifts floated down to outstretched public hands during time-outs. The team mascot known as The Grizz – a man in an 8 foot Grizzly Bear costume - fired yet more presents into the crowd with what was apparently the world's most powerful air rifle. There was rumour of midgets dressed as Elvis doing slam-dunks off a trampoline, but disappointingly this didn't transpire.

The call finally came on Sunday. 'I will be there in two hours,' came an unexpectedly eastern European voice. Holy crap! After five days of no word I'd all but given up on the immediate chances of Expedition Number 6, but suddenly all systems were firing. Apparently the truck upon which Priscilla the Bikecar was loaded had needed a parts replacement somewhere in deepest Montana, but all had been fixed and now was within touching distance of the Memphis suburbs. Rod, Dale and his granddaughter Bella listened to the news with wide, excited eyes. We were almost ready to roll. Now this journey was actually about to happen I had to make a video diary, update my website and then hope that the Bikecar itself was in good condition.

'The guy in Eugene said he rode it to the shipping post,' Rod told me, 'so it has to be in half decent working order.'

'Well, it's almost here, so we're about to find out,' I said, holding up two crossed fingers to my Canadian friend.

'Nothin' to worry about,' piped up Dale, 'anything becomes simple if you understand it.'

Dale's house was hidden in a confusing web of roads and cul-de-sacs so we drove out to meet the truck driver closer to the highway outside of Bartlett, Memphis. And there was Priscilla, finally, right up at the front of a vehicle transporters' lower deck. It was really quite funny, seeing this bizarre contraption, skinny and simple, amongst a collection of brand new shiny automobiles. The thought of having to unload all of the vehicles quickly abated with a little heaving and manoeuvring and after half an hour the Bikecar was off the truck and on the ground.

I'd seen pictures and videos but this first physical meeting brought instant reality to the challenge ahead. Such an unfamiliar, unsettling sensation overcame me, like I'd just met a good friend but had no recollection of her. I couldn't balance the fact that we were about to share so many memories, but she was so foreign. On a scale of good to bad, my mechanical knowledge is chronic. I've probably travelled further on roads than anyone else without a driver's licence, but not one flat tyre had occurred during 1,400 miles on a tandem bike and wheel changes were few and far between even during 4500 miles on a skateboard. Looking at the Bikecar, though, it was clear that there were a few parts that would require maintenance, at the very least. It's not that I mind getting my hands dirty, just that I prefer simplicity on a journey. The fact that I couldn't even begin to twist my mind around how Paul Everitt had conjured up this incredible machine with a combination of scrap metal, know-how and pure imagination in his garage, well, I was totally out of my depth.

Despite my inner lurchings, there was something effortlessly cool about Priscilla the Bikecar. She had the footprint of a small car but the chassis was nothing but a rectangular aluminium frame with a traditional bicycle wheel on each corner. Two of the tyres were flat. There were two worn-out white leather seats on the front, although I knew in a former life there had once been another two seats at the rear, like your average family car, except everyone was pedalling. The most recent iteration of the Bikecar didn't have the rear seats, and in their place was a battered old blue roof box, still covered in Paul's sponsor decals and other stickers he'd picked up on his crossing of Canada the previous year. The passenger-side chain didn't look like it had functioned for a while, something I definitely wanted to fix in order to have the option of company on the ride. The steering column extended to some bicycle handlebars in front of the left-hand front seat, which two days later would become the first driver's seat I'd ever take to a road on. I plonked down on the passenger seat and stretched out with a 'Hello Priscilla! Are you ready for an adventure?'

*   *   *

I hadn't spent a minute thinking about this project beyond checking on Google Maps to verify the distance between Memphis and Miami. If you plan anything to death it should come as no surprise that the life is sucked out of it, and I wanted the expedition to be endlessly reactive and spontaneous. A brief snapshot of how life can be if you just say yes. No voracious route planning, no flight at the end to get stressed by, no expectations, just adventure.

Not only was this trip always going to be a by-the-scruff-of-the-neck type of affair, but such was the possibility that the Bikecar might never arrive I had almost resigned myself to it *not* happening at all. So, it was with great surprise and delight when that call came from the truck driver on the evening of Sunday April 22nd 2012, and it was only then that the project began. I thought for five minutes then trotted downstairs and filmed the first YouTube video episode of an online series, which would go on to trace the story of one man and a bicycle that desperately wanted to be a car. It was titled 'The Waiting Game.'

The next 40 hours were a whirlwind. Priscilla could have been in better nick, but she could have been worse, too. Our group of friends in Memphis clustered, help offered from all quarters, a truly epic combination of skills, ideas, labour and on-the-spot planning bringing together the early stages of what I hoped would be one of the most memorable – if not bizarre – journeys of my life. Rod had spent years as a bicycle courier in Vancouver - I still remember his raised eyebrows when I revealed that I'd never changed a tyre, just hours before my first long distance pedal – and his experience was proving priceless.

He prowled around Priscilla on that Sunday night, making notes on what she needed and what parts were already hiding in the storage rack, which also needed replacing. Meanwhile, I stared in awe and befuddlement at the construction: the wobbly steering mechanism, the seats that looked like they'd been attacked with a lawn mower. Before me was a life-size version of a car made out of technical Lego.

I imagined the face-blistering gust from a swift downhill, could feel the stickiness of the Gulf rising up over a Florida road, the addictive, naughty scent of fuel-stained gas station air. Had you asked me eight years earlier what I might consider to be the epitome of adventure my response would almost certainly have been a heart-breaking cliché – climbing a mountain, visiting the Taj Mahal, walking the Inca Trail – and then I would have gone outside and cleared up Tikka and Korma's chicken shit from the yard with a low pressure hose.

Now though, things were different. I'm pretty sure that I'm the one in charge of my grand plan, but without even knowing it I'd become a grown man who was free enough to accept a 4-wheel pedal car from a stranger, then forge the blueprint for an unforgettable journey within three simple months. If this was how my adventurous nature was developing, I was delightfully content with my lot.

Prioritising factors from *Essential* to *Should Be Done* to *Would be Nice* makes the difference between reaching a goal on time, or reaching it three weeks late. Priscilla needed some work, this was clear. It was critical that my driver's chain was in good working order, with sufficient gears to allow me to both climb hills and achieve a half-decent pace on the flat. Brakes were important, the old girl weighed close to a quarter tonne and I didn't fancy a smash. We required at least two new tyres and the passenger-side chain needed rebuilding, but gears on that side weren't quite as important. And more important than anything, I needed a new seat.

We loaded Priscilla onto Dale's flatbed trailer and drove downtown to Tom Roehm's Big River Engineering shop. Tom was a tall, kind man with a brain capable of comprehending a solution to a non-evident problem before I could say, 'it all looks okay to me.' I'd asked Tom to help construct a new driver's seat. The one Paul had used across Canada was dirty, falling apart, and seemed ready to detach itself from the Bikecar at a moment's notice. Tom took some measurements, hummed a bit and then said, 'Leave me to think, bring it back in the morning and we'll get it sorted.'

Next stop was Outdoors Inc. Outdoors is an independent chain of Memphis recreation stores owned by the indomitable Joe Royer, who for almost three decades had fought off all competition from bigger outdoor stores who wanted to add Memphis to their catchment area. As well as boats, clothing and camping they had a bike department and we hoped, at such short notice, that they'd be able to tune the Bikecar up in a couple of hours. Outdoors Inc. staff not only love their job, but they tend to be good at it too. When Kenny and Andrea saw the Bikecar for the first time and then heard about my intentions for it they immediately went inside and reshuffled their schedules, eager to start their week off by fixing one of the weirdest contraptions they'd ever seen.

With Priscilla in good hands Dale, Rod and I drove around picking up food, a beer present for the Outdoors staff, and flags and stickers I'd sent off for printing earlier that day. A round robin email had resulted in a second hand but looked-like-new roof box from Mike Watson, who had paddled with us for the final four days of the Wolf River Expedition. 'Is it big enough?' Rod queried, and Dale, who is the most sprightly, excitable and lively mid-seventy-something I've ever met, obliged by crawling inside and pretending to have a nap.

'Would you now feel comfortable pedalling this to Miami?'

'That would be a tall order…by yourself it would be tough.' Kenny and Andrea had been working hard on the Bikecar but still seemed a little sceptical about the potential for my upcoming effort. Personally, I didn't have too many doubts. A test drive around Outdoors Inc. showed that the pedals, chain, gears and steering were all in working order, and as everyone knows, if you can pedal a Bikecar around a building you can pedal it 1,000 miles from Memphis to Miami, assuming the pedals, chains, gears and steering don't break. We drove back to Dale's house to pack, relax and prepare for a traditional Memphis farewell, which involved a pit fire in the garden, lots of people from all over town, a little bit of beer and some phenomenal food courtesy of Dale's wife Meriam, who was right up there in the top five as the world's best host. Eventually I fell to sleep, belly full and mind wandering, absolutely no idea what the next day would have in store, except for one thing: it would be the first day of yet another huge adventure.

12

Starting With A Bang

'It's a testament to English design,' Tom laughed at the Bikecar, 'a little duct tape every morning is all you need!'

Along the sidewall of the Big River Engineering loading bay, directly in front of the bright yellow stand up paddleboard that had seen 1500 miles of Mississippi River the previous year, were a choice of six potential seats. A $12 deckchair from Walgreens. A sturdy looking office chair with string slats. A larger, more durable garden chair. Then there was the old Bikecar seat with more duct tape around it, a lightweight camping chair, and a cast iron tractor seat, 'this'll make a man out of you,' Tom chuckled, heaving it off the ground.

After some thought we made a decision, the office chair would be the main seat and I'd take the Walgreens mini deckchair for emergencies. Tom set about the task of attaching the office chair to the chassis, while Rod and Dale bolted the roof rack to the back end of the Bikecar. I pottered around not doing a great deal except for taking film and harnessing nerves. Before me a shell was taking greater shape, the journey was almost upon us and all the fears I'd been suppressing bubbled to the surface. I needed to take a walk.

I was carrying a sensation that I'd never felt before, a strong sense that of everything I'd ever attempted this was the one journey most likely to fail. Just two weeks earlier my friend Sean, the photographer for the cover of Date, had his round-the-world cycling attempt delayed after being run over less than two hundred miles from Memphis. Despite concussion, torn thigh muscles and a fractured spine he had managed to resume his journey, but he was lucky. He wasn't the only British adventurer to find trouble in America either; Jason Lewis, Mark Beaumont, James Cracknell and James Golding had all been struck by vehicles whilst cycling in the USA: the odds of a ride without incident were not good.

I was terrified of traffic. The Bikecar was five foot seven inches wide and although, arguably, it provided a little more protection than a standard two-wheel bicycle it still wouldn't be much of a match for a motor vehicle in the event of a collision, and my lack of manoeuvrability meant I'd be at the mercy of drivers. Safety is a compromise for the beauty and freedom that a road trip delivers and while I felt the Bikecar would add an extra element of spice to this journey I also knew its width would increase the chances of an accident.

Compared to Europeans, Americans have a horribly dangerous culture of texting while driving and with relatively few people cycling the roads in the South any kind of bicycle, let alone a Bikecar, would not be expected by drivers. With two tall flagpoles and large reflective panels and tape on Priscilla's rear I was satisfied by my vehicle's visibility, but you're only visible if someone is looking. It takes one lapse in concentration, one dropped iPod, one quick glance down at a phone or a GPS, and at the wrong moment it could spell the end of a life.

Throw into the mix my ineptitude at anything bicycle-related and what can only be described as an irrational hatred for the thought of dealing with a flat tyre, and I was genuinely concerned about the chances of the journey being a success. There were so many excuses not to do this, so many potential flaws and dangers, so much doubt and inability that calling it all to a stop would have been the easy choice. But I held on to the only certainty in the entire plan; that the fears told me that this journey would give me experiences and memories that I'd never otherwise have.

I expected a hard, gruelling few days over the rolling hills of Mississippi and Alabama, and then, theoretically, the land would level out as I reached the upper edges of the Gulf of Mexico, and Florida. Just the thought of all the roads, hills, forests and vistas that I'd never seen bumped my caution slightly out of picture. Whatever happened, this was going to be one hell of an adventure.

*   *   *

'One of you has lost their office chair,' I rhetorically questioned the men gathered around the workshop, 'who is it?!'

A hand raised meekly, as if he'd be forever resigned to working from a garden lounger.

'You're a braver man than I am,' said another man, a wry smile on his face.

'Is brave the right word?'

'No,' he replied without a pause.

'I think it's going to be hot,' said the chairless man, shaking his head.

'So, the heat is the worst thing you think I'm going to face?' I pushed,

'No!' They all chimed in, '... bad drivers.' More shakes of the head, 'Good luck,' they said, their cheerful voices contradicting the alarm bells given away by their words and furrowed brows.

I turned to look at Priscilla just as Tom tightened a final bolt on the new chair, 'I'm very proud of you for taking this on,' he said, grinning, 'and I think you'll need these tools.' As he waved a bunch of spanners and wrenches in the air I resolved not to tell him that I wasn't overly familiar with any of them. He pushed them into my hands. In exchange for any fresh adventure you have to accept that there will be new skills to persevere with along the way.

An hour later a small group of people gathered in a car park beneath an overhead tram that silently glided people across a small channel to the Mud Island River Park. We were metres away from the historic Cobblestones, once the Memphis landing point for incoming ships preparing to pick up cotton, lumber and other local produce in exchange for cobblestones, which had been used as ballast. The landing has now fallen into disrepair but I'll always remember it for the scene of my arrival the previous year, accompanied by that wonderful crowd of paddlers. Since forming Expedition1000 I'd had a vision of twenty five different expedition tracks taking shape on a map of the world, each one at some point intersecting with another to form a higgledy piggledy route around the globe. On this day the newest of my routes was due to start where another had passed by, continuing the slow accumulation of connecting lines my trips were creating. Another network was evident in that car park: a circle of friends now ensuring they were more than just one-off faces in my life, happily chattering, snapping photos and preparing to send off a most unexpected journey. We gathered for a photo, Tom Roehm and Richard Sojourner ready with their bicycles, Dale preparing to drive his van and trailer behind us for the day so as to shelter us from Memphis traffic, Rachel Sumner behind the camera, Mike Watson and Linda Weghorst in support. It was time to go.

*   *   *

There's no way I could have started this journey without the skills, support and kindness of others. In many ways it felt like the hardest challenge had already been completed but as Rod and I pedalled our way from the banks of the Mississippi, through Downtown and out into the countryside we had no idea what would await us just a few miles out of the city.

Such had been the rush of preparation I was struggling to believe that we were finally underway. After five miles, still licking the southern Memphis suburbs, a tinkling on the road beneath us preceded our first breakdown. It appeared that all the rivets attaching my crankset to the gearing cogs had disappeared. There must have been only one or two remaining and our initial inspections had missed them – it seemed unlikely that all six had fallen out simultaneously, so Rod started to 'borrow' rivets from elsewhere on the Bikecar and plug them back in. Without them the crankset would have wobbled constantly, ensuring the tension on the driver side chain wouldn't be sufficient to keep it on the cogs. We'd managed to explore this first mechanical let down in what might be termed 'a rough part of town.' Locals eyed us closely, leaning up against doorframes and cars. I tried my best to look friendly and helpless, which summed me up very well, as it was Dale and Rod lying on the ground getting grease under their fingernails. I filmed them, silently thanking GoPro for making a camera so small it might not attract the magpie-like attention of the gangs around us.

Eventually we were ready to go again and we stopped only once the next hour, receiving a $20 donation from a farmer who couldn't quite believe what he was seeing. 'Rather you than me,' he chuckled, 'good luck!'

Rod and I had lapsed into an endurance-led silence, both of us pumping away at the pedals, focused on eating into the miles ahead. The delays of the last week meant that this was the only day Rod could enjoy on the Bikecar before his flight back to Canada, so we drove hard in order to get as far as possible with his assistance. A steady headwind pressed our faces and we spoke little, we'd reached our zone, there was a job to be done. Highway 61 arrowed straight towards the horizon beneath a blue sky littered with stretched out cotton bud clouds. Visibility was high and despite the traffic running endless and thick the protection offered from Dale behind us was comforting.

Then the illusion was broken. Resonating high above the background monotony of vehicles came a terrible, chilling screech of brakes. Hopeless, mournful screaming. Time slowed right down. Both Rod and I probably quit our pedalling although I can't be sure. I stiffened, tight in preparation for impact. A sickening crunch of metal marked the approach of what could only be imminent grief if I trusted the unstoppable rage of sound behind. Dale had been hit. It was our turn next.

The Bikecar was a sturdy beast, thick beams of heavy aluminium formed the chassis, but the velocity at which events behind us were unfolding meant that we were at the mercy of fate. All at once, milliseconds after the vehicles behind us collided, something hit us. A firm, uncompromising thud, instantly altering our direction, lifting the rear left of the Bikecar off the ground and throwing us off the road. It sounded like rushing water, sheaves of corn being stripped bare by the front fender and pedals as we careered down a verge. I was certain there would be a drainage ditch before the field flattened out as there had been one for many of the previous miles, but somehow the gradient levelled and eventually the corn brought us to a standstill.

'Are you okay?' For a moment Rod and I remained seated, staring forwards in shock. Then, as we turned to face each other he nodded, climbed out of his chair and left my field of vision. 'Jesus,' I whispered, checking my legs and feet for injury. There was none. My heart was thumping against its ribcage and it brought me out of a trance. Instinctively I reached forward, unclipped the waterproof case fixed to my handlebars, retrieved the camera and made my way up the hill to the road.

The air was filled with the blaring of a stuck horn. Three vehicles formed a triangular picture of the accident. Priscilla the Bikecar lay still in a field thirty metres off the highway, faint tracks leading off the road through grass and then crop betrayed her path. Straight up the verge a silver saloon angled across the hard shoulder, facing the wrong way up the highway. Dale's van and trailer seemed fine at first glance, he'd maintained control and parked half on the shoulder, half on the grass. I reached the top of the verge.

Rod was doubled over in attendance to a middle-aged black woman who remained in the saloon's driver's seat. His posture didn't suggest urgency so I turned towards Dale, who was out of the van inspecting the damage. 'Are you okay?!' I asked, putting a hand on his shoulder,

'I'm fine, how about you?'

'I'm fine, are you sure you're alright?'

'I'm good, there's nothing wrong with me at all.' Dale was perfectly calm and lucid, leaving me in no doubt that he was unhurt. As we turned around Rod was helping the other driver out of her car, and although she complained of a sore face from a deployed airbag she stressed that she too was okay.

'I'm so sorry,' she said, bending over with her hands on knees, 'I tried to get out of the way.'

13

Still Smiling

Two eyewitnesses joined us at the scene as Police and Highway Patrol cars pulled up, cordoning off the right-hand lane and immediately beginning a routine that seemed to be well practiced. I wandered around the vehicles, soaking up what had happened.

The front right of the woman's car was ripped apart from where it had collided with Dale's van. On the left side there was a deep dent on the driver's door where it had struck the back left wheel of the Bikecar. A smaller mark was on the rear passenger door on the driver's side where the car had appeared to graze my seat, which explained a slight soreness in my left shoulder and the silver paint now ingrained in the office chair installed earlier that day.

The car horn was still stuck on full volume, blaring out across scattered debris and black skid marks, which stretched 60 metres back up the road, telling a story that conflicted with my initial assumption that Dale's van had been knocked into us after being hit directly from behind.

She had been speeding, of that there was no question. Although our pace, of course, was far less than the average vehicle on Highway 61 that day, the flashing lights on Dale's van and trailer were clearly visible on a long straight road.

Sadly she didn't see him until it was almost too late. She had swerved left, dodging the trailer just in time but losing control after the swift movement. Over compensating, she lost control and the car began to spin clockwise. Her front right punched a deep cleft into Dale's driver-side door and front left wheel, a collision which encouraged her rotation. The Bikecar was next. Now facing the complete opposite direction to all other vehicles southbound on Highway 61, she struck our back left wheel, the main impact that sent us off the road. Before we went down the verge her car, velocity finally diminishing, bumped the side of my new chair, freshly extracted from someone's office at Big River Engineering. It was a miracle that no one had been hurt.

Had the impact come from a slightly different angle the Bikecar could have been flipped over, in which case Rod and I would have been left with no protection at all. The car could have easily rolled at that speed, possibly coming down on top of us. The collision had occurred directly in between the evenly placed telegraph poles along the roadside, meaning there was nothing solid to block our safe path into the field. So lucky. So lucky.

Although no fault seemed to rest with us I was wary of America's innate litigiousness, and sought to clarify the official position. As the policeman in charge matter-of-factly took statements from each of us, he told me he and his partner had seen us earlier in the day and assumed we were a charity journey or something similar. 'The fact you had a support vehicle suggested you were safety conscious,' the officer told me, 'if we'd have had any doubts about you being on the road we would have stopped you then.'

Once the police had collected their reports and moved away to make notes on the state of the vehicles the mood lightened.

'I'm so glad y'all not hurt,' said the woman driver.

'Well we're glad you're not hurt,' comforted Rod,

'I'm not hurt,' she confirmed.

'You're not in any shock?' I tested,

'No,' she shook her head, 'and you know, I've been having chest pain for two days, I should not have been on this highway.'

'Has this solved it?' I asked cheekily, always happy to break a dismal mood with some risqué humour. Quiet laughter rippled among the group and thankfully the woman smiled,

'I think so,' she chuckled, 'if I didn't have a heart attack then... yes...'

I moved down the hill with one thing on my mind. I found my phone in Priscilla's storage box then stood next to the now warped rear left wheel, which curved banana-like in retirement. I needed to make a call, pressed some buttons and felt the phone hold silent before ringing.

'Hello?' came a familiar voice.

'Hey you,' I said, my voice trembling.

'Is everything ok?' Emily asked, she knew immediately that something was up.

'Everything's ok now, yes, but we had an accident. A car hit us off the road.'

'Oh DC,' she said calmly, 'I'm so glad you're alright, thank you for calling me.'

'I just needed to hear your voice, and wanted to tell you not to worry if you saw anything online.'

'Thank you for calling lovely one,' she paused, then said, 'these things happen for a reason.'

I remained silent, focused on those words. It felt like a strange, unexpected thing to hear, but the manner in which she said it was so soft, so calm and so strong I couldn't help but be reassured. More than anything, she was the first person I considered calling and she'd answered right away. She was there for me. *My rock*. I digested this, standing near a busy highway accident scene next to a Bikecar, in a field of corn that gently swayed in the wind.

*   *   *

The last thing I wanted to do was to get back on the Bikecar and continue the journey. My worst fears had held true after just four hours on the road and 18.6 miles on the GPS, this had to be some kind of record! I'd always thought the last miles of an expedition were the most dangerous?

My call to Emily had been the first step in what needed to be a fairly fast decision about what would be my next move. Continue, or call it quits? Risk further incident with possibly greater consequences or do the sensible thing and relinquish the project? First impressions – based purely on the twisted wheel and the impact we'd endured - were that the Bikecar may need a great deal of work and investment to become road-worthy again, but my greater concern was for safety. If I did continue how many close shaves would there be? How many bumps, incidents, accidents? My viewpoint was biased with so much scattered wreckage strewn along the highway, but it seemed so unlikely that the road to Miami could possibly be clear from here on.

This was the first incident of its kind that I'd had on any of my journeys. I'd had a hairy time at the top of the Murray but it had been completely my fault, and a truck crash in South America had been bloody and traumatic but came long before my career and life choices were based around adventure. I was a different creature now, this moment was a marking stick for who I'd become.

Myself and Rod had been incredibly fortunate to have escaped with our health but this was my decision now, Rod was heading home and he was glad about it. Even if the Bikecar had been in working order he'd called time and I didn't blame him, this was one of those false fears that didn't diminish in stature when faced, it was very real indeed. Another aspect of chance was about to aid my thought process. Just three minutes after the accident a motorcycle pulled up, the rider clad from head to toe in black leather. As he removed his helmet I recognised him immediately;

'Do you remember me?' he asked, stretching out a hand.

'Jamie,' I smiled, 'good to see you mate.'

When I passed through Memphis the previous year

Jamie Zelazny had been present at a lecture I'd given at the Mud Island River Park. In the brief time we had to talk afterwards he told me he'd been a support kayaker for long-distance swimmer Martin Strel's journeys down the Amazon, Mississippi and Yangtze rivers, three expeditions that each deserve their place in adventure folklore. Jamie's attitude towards fixing a problem so the journey could continue was about to prove critical. At the roadside on Highway 61 Jamie told me he'd been aware of my Bikecar trek but had assumed I'd be taking a different route out of Memphis, so it was by complete chance that he'd witnessed the immediate aftermath of our crash when returning from work in the opposite direction. 'What's the problem with the Bikecar?' he asked.

'It's hard to tell,' I shrugged, 'we took a beating, but this wheel is pretty dead.' I tapped the culprit.

'Well, let's see what we can do,' Jamie prompted, 'I might have the right tools with me.'

Before any work could be done we had to get Priscilla out of the field. She was rolling well considering the damage but just as we reached the top of the verge we nearly collided once again with the silver saloon, which was now attached to a reversing tow truck set to remove the car from the scene. Jamie seemed content with the tools that he found in his motorcycle and eagerly set to work removing the damaged rear wheel and replacing it with a fresh frame and tire.

As he did this I chatted to Rod, trying to determine the best course of action. As the crash happened he had turned to see the car spinning towards us, a vision I was lucky enough not to have in my mind, and as a result his shock was far greater than mine. He was trembling, clutching in his hands a long-limbed teddy bear made from boardshorts that once belonged to a 14 year-old boy named Jesse Healey, who had been killed whilst riding his bicycle in Rod's home state of Ontario. Rod had subsequently orchestrated an annual memorial walk to promote bicycle safety and Jesse the bear travelled with him on all of his adventures.

Leaning against the van door, Rod talked about the suffering that had been left behind by a single, unnecessary incident, 'too much pain man, too much pain,' he repeated, slowly breaking down. This guy was made of much tougher stuff than I and his compassion ran deep, I was proud to be his friend and was sorry that our time on the road had come to a premature end.

Our time perhaps, but not mine. An immediate decision wasn't necessary, but it wasn't long before I made it. Jamie had replaced the wheel and it was spinning freely, suggesting the rear axle had avoided damage. Had we gone back to Memphis there's a chance that the slow process of mending Priscilla would have given memories of the accident a chance to grimly invade my mind, casting further doubt. But more than fear, I felt potential loss of a small part of my future. There are two ways to go after an incident like this. One: walk away. Two: realise that these things can happen but that possibility isn't cause to stop. Was I going to go home just in case something else went wrong or was I going to continue nevertheless?

The question had been valid before the accident, before the journey, before the Wolf and before The Sail. It had been posed before every expedition I'd ever taken; by myself and others. Risk is given as an implicit part of life but I felt bound to the knowledge that the experiences I'd gain by pedalling this strange four-wheeled contraption across the American South would improve me as a human, regardless of the presumed danger.

At that roadside I chose not to compromise my way of life simply because I feared the worst, and instead I would continue living fully, because without this attitude I may as well lay down in a box immediately. If my time is cut short, let every second up to that moment be rich, else my Mother once went through some hideous pain to deliver a child who would grow to waste his potential. And as my Mum is a passionate and vocal midwife always keen to share stories of her work, I have full intention to justify the suffering she went through to have me. I was a large baby after all; it would be rude of me to just graze my way through life.

'Let's get off this road and drive to the nearest town,' I said to the guys, as I climbed into the van's passenger seat, 'I'll continue on back roads from there.'

Dale wrestled with his driver's door, pulling it towards him several times before it shut. He paused, staring at it, then forwards and finally to his right towards me, before breaking into a beautiful grin, 'Still smiling,' he said, 'are you still smiling?'

I nodded.

'Me too,' he continued, 'it takes more than this to get me down.'

'I'm down,' said Rod, who was sprawled in the back of the van.

'All warmed up?' Jamie asked me, pulling on his biking gloves, 'start working those legs.'

'Yeah, well, the last thirty metres I didn't have to pedal at all,' was about all I could say. It was time to get back on the road.

14

Vicksburg

As night fell we drove to the nearest town, Tunica. Dale struggled at the wheel, the crash had clearly damaged the steering mechanism but he held course well. We'd been on the roadside for over two hours and the afternoon's events had left us exhausted and hungry.

We found a cheap restaurant and ate in near silence, then moved outside to unload the Bikecar from the trailer. Priscilla felt stiff and heavy but we circled the car park easily enough, a sufficient test run to confirm that movement was possible. With whispered thanks I bid a solemn farewell to Dale and Rod, not knowing when I would see them again, then Jamie led me through quiet, pitch black backstreets to a church, beside which I made camp on a patch of grass.

*   *   *

However hard things seem there are few quandaries that a good nights sleep can't begin to medicate. The next morning I rose early, keen to banish the memory of the day before.

Slowly, in a grand correlation with my speed that day, I realised that I wasn't ready to be back on the road. The front left wheel of the Bikecar had a very slight buckle. By 7am the Mississippi Delta was already providing a mighty show of its famed southerly winds, a blow to my already weakened mind. I'd hoped that conditions would remain clear until at least mid morning in order to allow accumulated distance to lessen the clouds in my head. Each mile that passed softened the edges of my paranoia yet yesterday's memories continued to haunt.

Every vehicle that loomed behind had me running scared. Three times in ten minutes I pulled violently off the road when a car approached without sign of overtaking, I was a ball of nerves, unable to enjoy an experience that usually I'd revel in. This was wide and flat land, enormous open fields either side of the road with little in the way to block the winds as they swept north from the Gulf. I was hitting an unmovable wall with each gust, my psyche less and less willing to drive me forwards.

For three hours at full energy I averaged no faster than 2 miles per hour. It didn't help that my seat fell off, with me on it. The impact from the crash seemed to have almost sheared the connecting bolts and just a few more miles of rattling along roads finished them off. Of course, the non-mechanic in me cowered at the probably small task ahead, my misery completed by the fact that the de-seating occurred right beside an elementary school. Small children lined up for break time attendance, staring at this strange white man affixing a flimsy pale green deckchair to a rather odd looking car. They must have thought an alien had landed. My shame was magnified when a teacher asked me to address the waiting pupils.

'Have you seen anything like this before?' I asked them.

'No,' came the universal response. I'm not sure whether it was directed at me, or Priscilla.

'It's called a Bikecar,' I mustered some gusto, 'it's a cross between two things, can you guess what they are?'

'A bike…and a car,' cheered the kids, excited, ending the game promptly.

I thanked the teachers and waved goodbye, then took off out of the gates at a miserly speed. In a parallel universe this would have been a moment of glory; children running and shouting alongside as this foreigner and his steed zoomed out of their lives as quickly as they'd arrived, but instead two lonely children walked ahead of me with hands in their pockets, clearly failing to comprehend how the combination of strong headwinds and instability of a rickety deckchair resigned me to permanent snail's pace.

Should the risk of accidents and failure deter us from embarking on these adventures in the first place? The risk of dangers can be lessened but should I have stopped riding I'd be giving up to the excuses I always made for myself in a past life. These things happen. If I stopped my adventures in a blinkered attempt to save my life, I'd simply be taking away my very reason for living. With all of that understood my head wasn't in a good place. Priscilla wasn't running smoothly and needed some work. I was sore and the headwinds were gusting up to 35 miles per hour.

I'd travelled 12 miles in 6 hours and wasn't enjoying myself. If I've gained anything from my adventures so far it's a deep knowledge of how I react in different circumstances, and along with safety my happiness is imperative. I wasn't happy, and I didn't feel safe. The final breaking point came when one, I could barely pull the Bikecar out onto the road after a short break, and two, the wind was blowing the Bikecar backwards faster than I could pedal it forwards.

By 5pm I'd travelled 15.2 miles, it wouldn't do. The smoothest the Bikecar was running was backwards when I climbed off - the wind just sailed it north. I've had low moments on journeys before but this took the biscuit. I have a lifelong ambition to become the first man capable of doing two things at once, which is why I set up engagements along the way during my expeditions. I had three days until the next one, but at 1.5 miles per hour I wasn't going to cover the 150 miles to Vicksburg, Mississippi in time.

The Bikecar needed work. I needed work. I needed rest. I decided to ignore the thoughts of an impure journey and go with gut priority, which was to sort out my state of mind. I was done, beat, exhausted, defeated. Day Two had compounded the events of Day One. I concluded that in order to look forward I needed to write the first two days off as a misadventure.

After a few calls my friend Tim McCarley agreed to drive north, pick me up and take me back to his hometown of Vicksburg, a few hours drive south. I'd have a few days rest, get the Bikecar properly mended then restart the journey once more. The distance to Miami would still be 1,000 miles so I wouldn't be jeopardising the journey's validity for Expedition1000 and besides, so much had happened already that this journey would be forever in my memory as Memphis to Miami. It wasn't a decision that I wanted to make but it was the right thing to do, I needed some time to shut off the screaming of that stuck car horn, which still rang deep in my ears and had me looking behind frantically each time a vehicle came along.

I just wanted sleep, a day of smooth passage, the ability to disallow visions that every driver on the road was texting or absent-mindedly grabbing for something under their seat. Just one mistake and it would be over. I wasn't ready to deal with that truth.

*   *   *

I rested for two days, clearing my mind of unwanted debris. The cathartic process of blogging and compiling videos about the start of the journey calmed me and reset my balance. I hid away in a sparse apartment above a huge, open plan garage that contained trucks and boats necessary for the operations of Dimco, a state of the art surveying and mapping company owned by Tim McCarley.

Tim had been one of the friendly faces that welcomed my brother and I off the Mississippi and into Vicksburg the previous year, and as part of my post-crash recuperation he intended to send me straight back to the river. En route to Vicksburg from the dusty roadside where Episode One of the Bikecar trip had unceremoniously ended, we had stopped in at the Quapaw Canoe Company in Clarksdale, Mississippi to pick up my faithful paddleboard Artemis, which I'd previously left in the good hands of renowned Riverman John Ruskey.

I'd originally chosen the southern route out of Memphis in order to reach Vicksburg in time for Tim's annual canoe race, the Bluz Cruz, and although things hadn't gone exactly to plan I found myself buzzing with excitement early on that last Saturday of April, darkness still untouched by sunlight as over one hundred people gathered in anticipation for a race down the Mississippi River. An hour later the starting point 22 miles upstream of Vicksburg became a riverbank of colour, a kaleidoscope of canoes and kayaks and one solitary yellow stand up paddleboard. A fierce headwind roared north and threatened to make my life miserable. After all, I was stood whilst all around me were seated, meaning I was effectively a sail. I was one of the final finishers in just under four hours but it was exhilarating being back on the big river, especially on such a wild day.

She was so wide it would take a full fifteen minutes to paddle across so 22 miles into a wind that largely negated any current was a challenge even for the best of the paddlers in the field that day. It was a splendid, timely reminder of our quiet inconsequence when faced with nature's power. The mood at the end of the day was humble and warm from exertion and accumulative effort. And it was with slight embarrassment that I collected a trophy for winning the event's first Stand Up Paddleboard section, having been the only paddler on a SUP that day.

Once the Bluz Cruz was finished Tim made getting the Bikecar ready a personal project and tinkered until late on Saturday night, trying to get his head around how the steering worked and where he could make improvements. I chatted to his daughter K.K, who in a tandem kayak with her Dad had finished high up the field in the race that day. Not yet halfway through her teens K.K was already an outstanding athlete, so much so that I declined when she asked me to go for a run with her, something about the certainty of being beaten by a girl forced me to protect my self-worth!

My feeling that every stranger is a friend waiting to happen was epitomised by Tim, K.K and their close Vicksburg community. Their Southern hospitality didn't just encompass offering accommodation and food, but involved them being an irreplaceable part of the journey. Time after time I am honoured to meet people like this, they teach me that giving is the best way to receive and that happy people don't necessarily have the best of everything, they just make the best of everything. In the South, they also fry everything, but let's not be picky.

Tim rolled around the front of the Bikecar on his own office chair, having just reattached mine to its rightful position in front of the handlebars. Then he set about playing with the wheels and steering mechanism. I produced my video camera, wanting to capture some of the rebuilding process. 'Tim, what are you up to?' I asked,

'We're going to get rid of all the slack we can get rid of and have much better steering and much better stability,' he informed me earnestly in his calm, perfectly Southern accent. He held up something metal, 'we took this silly metric bolt from the UK out and we're replacing it with this nice seven-sixteenths American standard rod...' A wide grin formed on his face, he was loving this. 'These modifications will make the journey much easier but we do have a guarantee Dave, guaranteed for one thousand and one miles. That's it though, anything over that, we're done.'

When Tim said '*done*' it came out as '*duurn...*' We both knew full well that his guarantee was strictly off the books, and that if I were to breakdown 500 miles away I'd still have to look after myself, but the game had been started, so I pressed him,

'Now, if I'm going really fast down a hill and it falls off...'

He cut me off. 'It's not my fault!' He laughed, 'it's not! Look! If you're going really fast down a hill after one thousand-point-one miles, you're on your own!'

Tim was a perfectionist as much as he was a fine host. He wasn't going to let me ride out without being fully satisfied with Priscilla's condition, and there's nothing like a stamp of approval from a good old English stereotype. He had straightened out some damage from the front right of the Bikecar, replaced the tyre, spun it smoothly and then looked up at me with wide, shining eyes. 'James Bond would be proud...and the Queen too!'

Shortly after K.K and I gave the Bikecar a test drive she bounded over to me with a sprightly, 'I got you some presents!' A bright green bandana was instantly promoted from my head to the flag pole on the back of the Bikecar, and she then fastened a bracelet to my wrist. 'It's camouflage,' she grinned, 'because that's what we wear in the South.'

15

Mile Zero

By the morning we were ready to go. Alongside Wayne Pratt, another Bluz Cruz organiser who had taken me to a Rotary lunch the previous week so I could share my story with the elder population of Vicksburg, Tim helped me load the Bikecar and push it up onto a trailer. Tim's work colleagues crowded around, curiously fascinated with this strange British man with a four wheel bicycle who proposed to pedal halfway across the country. I don't know if it was intentional, but the ones who weren't leaning up against motor vehicles bounced car keys in their hands, a subliminal reminder that they preferred their own transportation. That said, they all wanted a reminder of Priscilla's visit, and I found myself in the bizarre position of being asked to sign a pile of items gathered together from around the building. Once my scribble had found its way onto baseball caps, pieces of wood and even a sheep skull, we got down to business.

Tim unfurled a map on top of the Bikecar's storage box and we all had a good hard look; it was time to plan a route out of here. There wasn't a great deal of optimism from anyone in the Dimco shed, short words of advice went from 'Big log trucks running that road,' to 'this country ain't flat, you got some hills to look forward to over there.' Thick, calloused fingers prodded the roads fanning out from Vicksburg and heads shook at each option. Usually I wouldn't take much heed at these situations, when a person's primary bit of advice is 'don't ride a Bikecar anywhere' you can't expect too much positivity or accuracy on follow-up morsels.

Wisdom comes from experience and when travelling without a motor expect no consistency even from friendly predictions of distance, danger, time or road conditions. Knowledge that was valuable to me, such as a road having a wide shoulder or a route avoiding big hills, wasn't even on the radar for someone used to travelling the same route in a car or truck. Where I went from here would be potluck.

Although a few days off the road had eased the stress caused by the crash, safety was still the highest of my concerns and I recognised a theme in every opinion about roads leading out of Vicksburg. They were all busy and dangerous. Seeing as the journey was beginning all over again I had the liberty of getting a lift out of town to a safer starting point so I turned to Tim and Wayne and said, 'let's go somewhere that sounds nice.'

Sounds nice doesn't necessarily mean *looks nice*. An hour later we found ourselves unloading at a gas station in Crystal Springs, Mississippi, a tiny little place that served no purpose other than being a tiny little place in between places of more importance. There was certainly no sign of the town's former tomato-growing glory; legend had it that Crystal Springs was once known as the Tomatopolis of the world, although whether this was a term only used by locals I can't confirm.

Still, for all the apparent emptiness of the place, for me that span of concrete alongside the sibling partnership of an Exxon and a Chicken Run was about to have a great deal of significance. This is where the journey would finally start all over again. I recorded the final moments on camera, Tim and Wayne helped wheel the Bikecar off the trailer and then went GorillaTape crazy, affixing flagpole, flags and bright-coloured bandanas to Priscilla's rear.

I wondered how the guys were feeling about this moment, they'd offered more than the epitome of Southern Hospitality and had become good friends, both insisting that they take the morning off work to send me on my way. They shared my worries about traffic safety and had both voiced concerns about the sheer effort it was going to take to pedal Priscilla such a distance, but here they were helping in any way they could. I couldn't have been more grateful.

'What do you think are the chances of me getting to Miami?' I asked as they stood beside the Bikecar, ready for the off.

'Ninety eight, ninety nine per cent,' Wayne smiled casually, a mild wind whipping at his hair and tie. He looked at Tim.

'I'll go in that range, yeah!' said Tim enthusiastically.

'That's pretty high considering what's happened so far,' I chuckled, questioningly.

'We're not worried about what happened,' replied Tim immediately to affirmative sounds from Wayne, 'we're out of that, we're durn, we're startin' again, ready t' roll.'

I was going to miss these guys. I jumped onto Priscilla and pedalled out of the station, across the highway and then banked left onto the southbound lane. Tim and Wayne tracked me for the first mile, filming from their truck, and then I pulled into a wide gravel shoulder, hugged them goodbye and waved as they drove away. Then I was alone. You know you're on a journey when you say goodbye to people who are better friends than just a couple of day's company should allow, but as their tailgate disappeared over the slight hillock that separated my position from the heart of Crystal Springs I felt at ease, because this was exactly what I'd been waiting for.

With caution and fresh optimism I considered everything that had brought Priscilla and I to this position. Meeting Paul Everitt in London, Rod's work to get the Bikecar to Memphis, the banding together of everyone in that city and then Vicksburg following the crash. And now here, ten minutes pedal from Mile Zero, all but a tiny fraction of the journey lay ahead. And as I looked along the road I was about to travel it seemed apt that my first challenge, almost immediately, was a bloody big hill.

*   *   *

Six years earlier I had knelt to kiss a solid white line painted across a road in Scotland that would eventually lead the length of Britain to Lands End, Cornwall. Taking the first few pushes of that journey I briefly let thoughts about what lay ahead infiltrate my mind and I felt so overwhelmed that by the top of the first rise, less than three miles from the start, I felt inclined to pick up my skateboard and resign the dream for good. Had I bowed to that momentary weakness I most certainly would not have found myself in a similar situation again, and I would have become a more desperate man for it.

Instead, I pushed Elsa the bright yellow skateboard for 34 days, over 896 miles, my first journey. It taught me that I could charge on and that self-belief was enough to overcome those hardest of challenges; staring down the road that travels beyond your imagination, beyond any previous point of will you've allowed yourself to cross. So daunting, seeking the unknown; yet so thrilling, finding the strength to take those first movements forwards.

After that first journey I had no more doubt. I developed my own ways of dealing with the thought of remaining miles, and mainly they involved never seriously considering the distance ahead. I'd break it down into days; reaching the next tree, small sprints to a landmark, incentivising myself further with small rewards like a cold drink in a petrol station or a new view around a bend; or a free coast down the hill whose brow once seemed so far off. I will never travel the same road twice, not slowly. Adventure is about the reward of newness and finding personal development in experience earned the hard way.

From my seated position on the Bikecar I loved that I had no idea what hid beyond that first hill and it gave me reason to spin the wheels. I sat back on Priscilla, but for the first time I was completely by myself. Nobody was waiting nearby or pedalling with me. If I was going to go anywhere I'd have be the sole motivator. I assessed my surroundings, ensured my beloved Aquapac rucksack was secure on the passenger seat, then began a ritual that would be repeated several times daily for the next few weeks.

I put on a $10 pair of knock-off Aviator sunglasses that I'd bought from the Exxon back up the road. They made me look like a policeman, so it was lucky that I was without a uniform, or a gun, or a proper car, otherwise people would have been confused. Took a sip of freezing coffee from a can then leant forward and adjusted my GoPro camera, which was attached to a bendy tripod wrapped around Priscilla's chassis in front of me. A little more coffee, it was hot out. A quick glance behind to check the traffic, the road was clear but I wasn't quite ready to get going yet. Reached forward and turned on my GPS, which rested just below my handlebars in what would usually be used as a runner's arm strap for an iPod. More coffee. I pedalled tentatively, edging nearer to the road, wheels slipping on the gravel beneath me.

The moment was coming, the road trip I'd dreamed of, but a rushing, roaring sound approached fast from behind. I pulled hard on the brakes; my left wheels still a couple of feet from the road. A log truck blared past, bringing with it a thick smell of fresh wood and a blast of hot air that grabbed at the hair creeping out of my helmet. I looked behind again, clear road now. Started pedalling, straightened out with Priscilla's right wheels licking the white line, and then hit the road in search of new adventures.

The view I'd longed for upon reaching the top of that first hill was unexpected. Hundreds of signposts of all shapes and sizes lined the frontage of a ramshackle property, signs reading Alcohol Kills, Tobacco Kills. Another one propped up against an old, abandoned yellow school bus read There Are No Christians in Hell. A belief is a belief but I imagined that the school bus was where they stored the bodies of people who stopped to look around.

The parade of signs warned of the imminent likelihood of the World's End and imploring all to follow God, otherwise he would smite them. It seemed like bullying to me and I'd be damned if the world was going to end so soon after getting the journey going again, so I pedalled on quickly before I was kidnapped. There was no shoulder but the road was quiet and cars passed infrequently. Every other vehicle was a log truck but they gave me good berth and sometimes a light and friendly tap on the horn.

In Vicksburg I'd affixed an old wing mirror into my

left-side handlebar, the glass in the mirror was broken but there were remaining pieces just big enough to give me clear vision and I checked it every few seconds to ensure I wasn't soon to be visited by another vehicle. As the morning drifted into afternoon I made small adjustments to the mirror, to the gears, to my sitting position, slowly becoming comfortable at the helm and appreciating the Bikecar's operating capacity. I revelled in the calm air, the Mississippi hills now guarding me from the delta winds that had haunted the first two days.

The Bikecar was heavy and took some work to move from standing, but on the flat we averaged between 6 and 8 miles an hour and although uphill was not easy the lowest gear allowed me to crawl forwards, finally earning a shallower gradient before the road flattened out at the top. For the first two hours I climbed without a single freewheel but I was fresh and any soreness from the crash was long gone. I was on a mission now, it was time to accumulate miles and cover ground. I tempered the monotony of my robotic feet with constant mathematical breakdowns of miles travelled, miles left, miles I'd need to average per day, miles to the next cold drink, average speed in miles per hour. Miles. And Miles.

I felt my calves and thighs burn with yet another hill but consoled myself with the knowledge that we were heading to the sea and that at some point every inch I had climbed would allow me a downhill run. There was little enjoyment to be gained from climbing but I knew it was exactly what my body needed to condition for the weeks ahead, especially considering I hadn't trained a bit for the journey. I've never really trained for a big expedition, figuring that growing fitness is simply a beautiful by-product of kicking ones ass for several hours a day in the process of getting somewhere new.

In fact, an utterly ridiculous realisation caught up with me after ten miles or so had logged on the GPS; before this journey had begun I hadn't pedalled any kind of bicycle for over a year, the last time being the final day of the tandem ride into Las Vegas. Training is for sissies.

We were running right through thick forest, the road itself the only sign of humanity except for the occasional property that I could only assume had been created for a horror movie set. Off the road there was always an almost-but-not-quite opaque line of trees split only by a dirt pathway leading to a tremendously broken house of wood, separated from an enormous and eerie barn by a dozen doorless, windowless, engineless cars.

There were never people in sight when I passed these scenes, only the menacing tinkle of pointless windchimes, perhaps a dog barking in the distance, the ubiquitous snarl of a chainsaw. People screaming. Okay, there were never people screaming but I imagined this was just because they were too weak to expend any more energy; it must be tiring being trapped in a redneck's shed. You might already be fearing for my sanity, it still being Day One and all, but this is how I kept myself entertained. And this is why I do these things, to escape from noise and to allow my mind to run wild as though I were a child once more.

Remember how simple it used to be back then? When we didn't have any responsibilities and we still believed in Santa and *anything* was possible. Our bravery wasn't limited by caution or our enthusiasm by expectation. Energy was boundless and unhindered by age or the subsequence of injury. We had less to lose and our imaginations were free. These were all sensations I sought to revisit as often as I could, reminding myself that I'll always be connected to the child I once was and that retaining some of this unbridled nature, if not innocence, would slow down my imprisonment to commitment and responsibility that so often line the edges of adulthood with grumpiness. The sheer absence of complication by setting the elementary goal of moving slowly towards a final destination reduces undue pressure and allows open creativity, thus enriching the journey and letting the experience thrive. Simplicity holds hands with happiness and as I pedalled south with few things to worry me the day improved along with the frequency of sweat beads dripping down my forehead.

The most beautiful view of the first day involved the road disappearing. I'd climbed for hours and suddenly I could see nothing but a thin passageway of horizon in between trees. The valley floor lay so far away it existed as a dull green beyond the afternoon haze, visibly lower than my position. *The road must run downhill for miles*, I thought to myself, instantly needing an excited pee. The brakes squealed wildly as I pulled over onto the verge and rushed through long grass to find a bush. Another of the simple pleasures of voyaging: the toilet is everywhere.

I made my way slowly off the highway and over the railway tracks, passing a few small, pleasant houses belonging to Wanilla, Mississippi. The road slowly turned to gravel and hard sand and I turned off as I saw a signpost for a boat ramp. I'd asked directions from a man a few miles back and he'd pointed me in this direction, with a 'Y'all fixin' to go durn there, there's a campin' place by the river…' And he wasn't wrong. It was a dirty river, nothing like the Pearl it was named after, but nonetheless, it calmly drifted by twenty metres below the rough old picnic shelter that stood quietly at the top of an overgrown, under maintained boat ramp.

It was a lovely spot to stay the night. I parked Priscilla

right under the shelter, slung my Sky Tent between two supporting beams, cobbled together some dinner from the supplies in my storage box, then had a good look at my map. In addition to covering a solid 32 miles and regaining the confidence in both Priscilla and the chances of my completing this journey without being squished, I had been buoyed by a phone call from Em during a mid afternoon gas station rest stop. She was now back in Miami and was planning a work trip to the Shedd Aquarium in Chicago, but she'd wangled a couple of days out to come and visit me. She was planning to fly into Pensacola two days later, then would hire a car to come and find me somewhere south of Hattiesburg, which meant that although my weary body was in much need of rest I had one heck of an incentive to cover the next 80 miles.

16

The Longleaf Trace

I rose before sun up, stretching out my limbs, toes and fingers, all sore from the previous day's efforts but ready to work again. Squirrels leapt from branch to branch above my head as I packed up camp, mist rising from the river painting a delicious haze across the fields. I eagerly retraced my route back into Wanilla, over the train tracks and onto the road I'd left behind the evening before, excited for what the new day might bring.

The air was delightfully fresh and it spurred me on through the open linear outskirts of Wanilla, bungalows set back a hundred metres off the road, growing into more disrepair the further south I pedalled. I was already becoming familiar with Priscilla's personal array of behavioural sounds, especially their ability to rouse the attention of dogs large and small. Luckily most of the properties kept their canines behind high fences, and I breathed a sigh of relief when I passed the last house in town having only had to evade the hungry snapping of three miniature terriers, which couldn't have reached my bum if they'd tried. I consider myself an animal lover but I've never seen the use in small dogs. Their only purpose is to bark pitifully and pretend to be bigger than they are, which appears to be a pointless existence.

Few vehicles passed in the first half hour and it wasn't until I branched left onto the busier Highway 84 that I encountered heavier traffic. A two-foot shoulder offered some security and the road was smooth, flat and well built, which in tandem with the still air and coolness of early morning made progress swift and enjoyable. I was revelling in the freedom of riding through fields and the realisation that the lack of a support vehicle blocking my rear view my wing mirror gave me full vision of any vehicles – and therefore potential danger – with enough advance time to make a judgement call. I could see whether I'd been spotted if the following vehicle moved away from the side of the road and into an overtaking position.

Out here, far from a dense urban area, it was rare that a car or truck would be required to slow down before overtaking because of another vehicle travelling in the opposite direction, but if this appeared too likely and if the roadside verge allowed me the freedom, I would simply pull fully off the road and let the vehicle behind continue in a straight line. I didn't want to be a hindrance to anybody and by adopting this simple etiquette I was unlikely to infuriate my fellow drivers, keeping karma on my side and blood running calmly through my veins.

All of this said, if I was offered a chance to ride on a quieter road I would have taken it, and this is why I was headed to Prentiss, Mississippi. Tim McCarley had made my day by suggesting that there was a cycle path leading to Hattiesburg, MS from Prentiss, but experience has taught me never to take such good news at face value. Tim admitted he'd never travelled along the path but told me that he'd heard that it was all downhill from Prentiss. I tried my best not to listen, my hopes would depend on those beautiful words and they seemed too good to be true.

I reached Prentiss in the early afternoon having covered over 25 miles, and sated my hunger and thirst in a Subway sandwich shop, where the air con was a welcome escape from an atmosphere thickened with heat, vehicle fumes and the constant scent of felled wood from logging plants alongside the highway.

The Longleaf Trace began unceremoniously, snaking away from a closed station and quickly leaving the low-level civilization of Prentiss behind. After a day and a half on roads I was overjoyed to have discovered the trace, having struggled to even believe it actually existed until I saw it with my own eyes. The path was more than wide enough for the Bikecar and although the first few miles were definitely not in keeping with the 'it's all downhill' rumours my pace was totally unhindered. It was just me, the path and forest either side, there didn't even seem to be any other humans around to get in my way. Like many other 'greenways' or cycle trails sprouting up across the United States this one followed a former railway line, and I vowed to track down as many of these rail-to-trail traces as I could in the coming weeks.

Adventure, like science, has a wonderful way of making one realise that what you previously thought was true and factual was simply knowledge keeping you comfortable until another explanation came along. I tried to reassure myself that the Longleaf, being a trail that followed a former train track, couldn't possibly continue uphill because trains operate best on the flat. But apparently this one didn't, because by the time the sun began to touch the horizon I hadn't yet enjoyed a single freewheel that lasted more than 3 seconds.

It was the first true mind game of the journey, sometimes the path's gradient was so imperceptible I couldn't tell whether my efforts were strained because I was on an uphill or that the Bikecar had a problem. Twice, I became so puzzled by this I stopped fully and only became satisfied that I wasn't crazy when Priscilla began to slowly roll back towards from where I'd come.

It had been a solid afternoon of steady climbing and I would have been forgiven for expecting to see snow at some point, but the ease of the trail had allowed me to almost double my lunchtime distance in just a couple of hours, bringing stark reality to the test I'd set myself. Pedalling Priscilla was a glorious, unique feeling, but it was always going to be a slow, steady plod, especially on main roads where I would frequently pull over to allow traffic to pass.

Thanks to Longleaf I managed to cover 48 miles on that second day and slung my hammock beside one of the regular pedestrian stations, ensuring I had a proper toilet and a place to fill up my water for the night. I wolfed down the remaining half of my Subway from earlier, stretched and settled down, hoping that my chosen campsite would not be disturbed.

*　　*　　*

Priscilla and I were on our way again by 7am on the third day, eager to reward some early miles with a good breakfast in Hattiesburg at the end of the trail. There was another incentive, Emily was due to fly into Pensacola mid afternoon and would reach our accommodation by dinner, I had to get a wriggle on.

Of slight concern was a sore left Achilles tendon and left knee, a leftover football injury from my University days that only ever bothered me when it was forced into a cycling motion. Such was the weight of the Bikecar I was aware that my legs were under considerable strain especially on uphill stretches, but I was more worried about snapping a chain, so on the few inclines where pedalling became near impossible I held the brake, climbed off and pushed Priscilla to the level again.

Small frogs were out, sunbathing in the middle of the path, and there were also many more cyclists the closer I got to civilisation, most of them looking at me in disgust as Priscilla took up much more of the trace than most of the other contraptions around. That they still had a metre or two to play with seemed more than fair - we all have wheels, we're family!

A familiar occurrence for any social media-savvy modern-day adventurer will be the unarguable ball ache of self-filming. My chief mode of story-sharing on this journey was YouTube and while I love translating my experiences into little pieces to camera and capturing the world from the level and speed by which I travel, there comes a time when you have to film from further than arms length. This often comes at a time when you're exhausted or about to tackle a gruesome hill, something that you want to get out the way as soon as possible but something that would also look cool on film. The procedure is simple but time consuming.

In the case of this journey I'd stop, park the Bikecar, walk forwards, mount a camera on a tripod, return to the Bikecar, ride on past the camera until I was satisfied with the shot. Stop, park the Bikecar, walk back and collect the camera before returning to the journey at hand. Whenever the Longleaf Trace reached a small village the path would cross over a road and I wanted to capture one of these crossings. I attached my GoPro to a magnetic tripod, clamped it right onto one of the Crossing Here signs then proceeded to ride over the road and down the path. Unbeknownst to me, on my return to grab the camera, Priscilla realised that she'd been left on a slight decline and it was only when I turned around that I saw her off the path and down a ditch. Luckily there was no damage but the resulting half an hour it took me to unpack the storage box and heave the empty Bikecar back up onto the path was only slightly remedied by the hilarious footage caught by my camera as I walked towards it, Priscilla in the background seeming to will herself into the neighbouring forest without assistance.

I reached Hattiesburg, Mississippi by 10am, and thus the end of the Longleaf Trace. For the best part of a day I'd been uninterrupted by traffic and I was sad to leave the path behind, but a familiar feeling overcame whatever sentimentality I was experiencing for the cycle path; it was well and truly time for breakfast.

I powered through town, past the University of Southern Mississippi stadium that is home to the Golden Eagles football team and eventually settled in a coffee shop called Southbound, which seemed apt. Tim McCarley had recommended that I get in touch with a 'switched on' young guy who ran the local Sacks Outdoors store but my phone calls had been left unanswered, so it was to my great surprise that as I entered the coffee shop a customer at the counter turned to me and asked, 'Are you Dave?'

In his mid twenties, Aaron Sackler was an enterprising chap and I liked him immediately, partly because he bought me coffee, toast and eggs. He'd grown into the family business and was responsible for the day-to-day running of Sacks, which somewhat like Outdoors. Inc in Memphis had managed to survive despite the threat of larger national chains taking custom elsewhere. 'I prefer the outdoors side of things,' Aaron told me, 'but we rely on industrial business to keep going, steel-capped boots are our biggest seller by far.' He shrugged, and conversation moved on to his efforts to bring Stand Up Paddleboarding to Hattiesburg, a town with little water to speak of.

I liked the guy, he was keen, honest and generous, and once breakfast was done we walked across the lot to his store, Aaron stopping to admire Priscilla en route, as she was parked in an entire parking slot to herself. Rain had begun to fall, making good on the forecast's promise for thunderstorms and threatening any comfort I may have had for the rest of the day's ride.

First, we popped into Sacks Outdoors and Aaron went into overdrive, asking, 'could you use a flashlight?' and, 'need any shorts?' Had I accepted everything Priscilla would have groaned under the resultant weight, but some insect repellent and a strong waterproof flashlight, along with some superstrong duct tape to affix the light to Priscilla's rear, were more than welcome gifts. I hugged Aaron goodbye and gave his staff the same treatment, and they all came to the door to see me off, their faces covered in pity as I donned Aaron's final present to me, a transparent waterproof poncho.

The rain streamed off the poncho into my lap as Priscilla's front wheels picked up the slick from the road and flung it into the air. The downpour had instantly torn up the muddy, dishevelled backstreets through which I rode, the Hattiesburg lower class staring in disbelief from their verandah sofas, foam busting out of aged seams behind their heads and legs. I went as far as I could on the back streets before being forced back onto proper road, visibility reduced considerably by the rain, which bounced up in a wall all around.

It really was filthy weather and by the time I reached an out-of-town gas station my appearance had become all the more unique. It seemed that all southbound vehicles had sought shelter at the Shell garage on the Highway 98 circular and a hundred pairs of eyes stared through rivulets of water on the misty café windows as I pedalled straight under the gas station overhang and into a free parking space under cover. A stream of inquisitive folk paused to admire Priscilla on their way in or out of the station, the conversations going something like,

'Where ya headin','

'Miami!'

'Are ya crazy?'

'Well let me ask you this, how much did you pay for gas?'

'Fifty bucks,'

'Then you're the crazy one!'

'Good luck son,' they'd say laughing, 'rather you than me.'

*   *   *

I had ten miles left to cover before my rendezvous with Emily and set out once the rain had calmed. I took a quiet road that rolled endlessly through green fields and forest, the air filled with the sweet perfume that only rain can induce from the land. My lungs were bursting with the accumulative effort of over 100 miles pedalled in two and a half days, as well as the merciless ups that followed the downs in this part of the world.

The wet roads meant that Priscilla gained less traction than in the dry and I found myself pushing her up many of the hills, but my mood raised when passing through the district of Dixie, when a sign next to a sport's field declared that this was the home of the 2005 Superbowl Midget Football Champions, listing not only the Midget players but the Midget Cheerleaders too. Gosh it made me giggle, even though I had a sneaking suspicion that in this part of the world *Midget* was just another term for *Youth*. It's the small things that get me.

My only other delay was a short chat with a man named Bill, who donated $4 to the charity coffers and had a dog named Shebuskin Shebuttons that spread all over his passenger seat like a polar bear. Bill told me how he had once been a marine, where his grown-up children lived, how their kids were doing at school and how he'd learned to swear like 'a proper man' during his first visit to Australia. 'They sure know how to drink down there, too,' he added.

Thirty minutes later I found myself turning off a tiny country road down a muddy driveway only to face a steep hill. I felt sure from the directions I'd been given that I was in the right place but just in case decided to walk down the hill and check it out, before driving Priscilla down and not being able to get her back up. Em had found this place online and prepped the owner for our arrival but I had no idea what to expect, so when I reached the bottom of the hill and caught a view of the Black Creek Cabin I was blown away. It was perfect, a vast wooden cabin raised fifteen metres off the ground on stilts. 'You're in the right place,' called a voice, which I located as coming from the body that had appeared up against railings at the top of the outside steps.

'Hello! Let me get my vehicle!' I shouted back, immediately scrambling back up the hill and bringing Priscilla down in a frantic sideways-skidding motion, splashing through the mini-lake that had accumulated at the bottom of the slope. By the time I reached the cabin the man, who introduced himself as Rusty, had descended the steps and was shaking his head at the sight before him, a wry smile on his face.

'I've seen some things in my time,' he chuckled, 'I can't wait to hear *your* story, Emily gave me the cliff notes but I have a feeling she didn't scrape the surface.'

Rusty helped me lift the Bikecar up onto the concrete foundation slab under the cover of the house, mud dripping down my soaking bare legs onto mud-covered shoes. As I quickly unpacked I told Rusty what brought me to Mississippi, on a Bikecar. I told him about being an awful graphic designer at the age of 25, quitting my job during a quarter life crisis and skating across Australia. I told him about forming Expedition1000, that this was the 6th journey, that I was trying to raise £1 million for CoppaFeel, how Emily and I had met. I told him everything in about two minutes and as he helped me lug my drybags up the steps he said, 'well, I thought this was going to be a special visit, but seeing as your reason to be here seems so valid, you'll be staying for free as my guest.'

17

Black Creek Cabin

Rusty gave me the tour and I made thanks for Em's Googling skills. She'd discovered the cabin online, a real find. An open plan kitchen and living space, two separate double rooms and a gorgeous deck looking down over the Black Creek itself, which bubbled happily on its way south. Outside, the rain was pouring down and lightning flashed across a dark, brooding sky. With a text, Em had told me earlier that she was driving through torrential conditions and had seen multiple cars wrecked at the side of the road. She'd pulled over to let the worst of the storm pass but was now on her way again, a little later than expected.

When we'd said goodbye in Hawaii our upcoming time apart seemed infinite, there was even a chance that Em might be out of Miami on work when I eventually arrived. Our relationship had always played out like that, rarely was a goodbye accompanied by certainty, but it was that openness that heightened anticipation of the next, often impromptu meeting.

Rusty noted my anxiety as I paced the lounge, both of

us sharing details about our lives as though we'd been friends for longer than twenty minutes. He was a supremely laid back character with an adeptness for sarcasm that belied his nationality. Ah, sarcasm, it probably shouldn't be a surprise that this humour-mutation struggled to thrive during the tough, exposed ocean crossings of Eriksen, Colombus and other Europeans who brought new culture to what would become the United States.

I liked Rusty for his honesty and his dry turn of phrase. He seemed to have a keen interest in why Emily and I spent our time as we did. He said that he wanted to meet her but would be out of our hair as soon as she arrived, but would perhaps pop back later to see how we were getting on. He didn't come close to being intrusive but I bristled unfairly, knowing that as soon as Em and I had the chance of time with each other we'd shut up shop, lock the door and disappear into our own world.

Then the sound of an engine growled and a car appeared across the clearing at the bottom of the muddy slope. Em!

Rusty stayed inside as I went outside to greet her. Her smile, now so familiar, was beaming as she trotted up the steps, blonde hair in waves about her face. I wrapped my arms around her waist and pecked her lips gently, 'Hello Blue Eyes.'

'Hello DC,' she purred, 'that was a horrible drive.'

'It was worth it I hope,' I smiled, 'come inside and meet Rusty.'

There were few supplies in the cabin so Rusty organised for his wife to deliver wine and a takeaway before he bid us farewell. His last words were, 'if you want to stay an extra night you'd be more than welcome.' Em and I thanked him, watched him leave, drew the curtains, and took each other's hands.

*   *   *

I was becoming accustomed to this. The terror so regularly felt at getting close to such a free spirit evaporated as soon as we were together. Nothing else mattered and no span of time was long enough; the only sadness was that we had less than a day before her next plane. 'You're flying an awful lot these days, considering you hate flying,' I winked at her.

'Well, perhaps I have my reasons,' she grinned, 'my parents are already wondering why I'm planning another

UK visit next month, I've been back more this year than in the past three.'

'And why are you planning another UK visit?' I pressed, eager for her to say the reason out loud, 'there must be something worth visiting so frequently.'

'Oh you know, it's mainly for the weather.' She giggled and brought her face close to mine, 'DC, what are we doing?'

'It's more like, what are we about to do?' I whispered mischievously, kissing her. I stood, picked her up and walked to the bedroom, trying my best not to bang her head against the doorframe.

*   *   *

The morning arrived too fast, but it brought sunshine. We bathed on the deck with coffee and eggs, briefly considering going for a dip in the Creek before I told Em that the riverbanks were perfect Cottonmouth snake territory. The plan worked perfectly. 'We should stay up here in that case,' she said, snuggling into me.

The time soon came for her to leave.

'I love you,' I told her, the words hanging in the air.

Then I lost my nerve, '…a little bit.' We'd had such a lovely night and here we were at the top of a set of wooden steps that would take her away from me. I couldn't tell whether she had disappointment or relief written on her face but there was one thing left in no doubt, we were interwoven.

'I'll try to come and find you in a fortnight,' she said with one final kiss.

'Drive safe please, little one,'

'You too.'

And then she was gone, her rental car tentatively scaling the slippery slope; purring out of sight across Mississippi.

I decided to take Rusty up on his offer to stay another night. The first three days on the road had left my body weary and an afternoon of video editing and diary writing matched a need for rest. Rusty and his three sons visited in the evening, a terrific group of lads, each very different but all personable and bright. The previous night I'd managed to snap the plastic corkscrew when trying to get into a bottle of red and we'd eventually given up on trying to dig the cork out of its hole. Rusty's sons took the matter in hand and somehow, remarkably, they managed to coax it out. I watched with a mixture of awe and embarrassment: like I said, I'm not good at the mechanical things.

'I was looking at your website, you've done some stupid

stuff,' said Rusty, his sideways glance catching my eye.

'Stupid is as stupid does' I replied, getting my Forrest Gump impression ready for Alabama, a State I hoped to reach in the next two days.

'And this girl of yours, she is incredible.' Rusty paused, 'How did *you* manage to convince her to spend time with you?'

'Bribes,' I said, shrugging, 'and wearing a paper bag over my head helped a lot.'

'Keep hold of that one, she's a knockout,' he said, solemnly, 'they don't come along like that very often.'

'You're telling me,' I nodded.

18

Alabama

I was away early, dragging myself out of a wide, comfortable bed made far easier with a consoling mug of coffee. The steepest hill of the journey so far presented itself less than a mile from the cabin and washed away any comfort I'd become used to on my rest day, but already I was feeling my fitness returning. My exercise patterns are either intense or non-existent. I've never been able to engage in a routine involving daily runs or visits to a gym so in between expeditions I go to pasture, spend much of my time in front of a laptop and incubate some fat. After a month of these fallow periods I notice that my fitness has departed, usually when I spy a fence or a small wall that just a few weeks back I could have happily jumped over, but now it just screams '*knee injury!*' I can afford these weeks or months of down time because another span of superbly intense physical activity is always around the corner, but man I love the feeling of regaining my health. It's empowering and gives me confidence socially, creatively and physically. I willed more steep hills to test me; I was ready for them once again.

I was just thinking that this part of Mississippi resembled English countryside when I rounded a bend to find the road covered in cows. There didn't seem to be much order to proceedings although hedgerows either side of the road channeled the cattle, however haphazard their navigation was. But one thing pulled me out of imagining that I was in my own country: a black and white sheriff car with flashing lights seemed to be acting as shepherd. A middle-aged lady rushed after the car and animals, slowing her pace only briefly to look at me and my own steed. 'They escaped!' she said, 'happens all the time.'

'Oh, are the police really herding those cows?' I asked,

'Yes, they're very good about this kind of thing, we're all neighbours.'

'This doesn't happen in England, not with the police at least!' I said, still amazed by this patrol car pushing 100 cows back from whence they'd come.

'It doesn't?' She asked, surprised.

'No!' I confirmed, adding, 'You better continue your chase, have a good day!'

'Same to you. We're glad you're visiting America!'

'I'm loving it!' I chuckled as she bustled down the lane.

Through social media I'd put out word that I was

looking for members of the public to join me but I didn't hold out much hope for an excessive number of co-riders. It's ever so difficult to find someone who both happens to be in the right place and is also willing to break from their normal schedule in order to join a ridiculous mission. But Rusty Easterling was just the man. He'd stopped in at the Black Creek Cabin to check that I hadn't left anything behind, then found me twenty miles further south just outside of a town named Wiggins, where I'd enjoyed a lunchtime nap under the shade of a maple tree. I'd curiously witnessed several romantic unions in the roadside park. Maybe it was my imagination, but it seemed strange that during my time there three different couples each met at this place, each partner driving up in a separate vehicle in dark glasses before scurrying quickly over to a another vehicle containing someone else they wanted to kiss. The Dizzy Dean rest stop outside of Wiggins, Mississippi appeared to be a lovemaking hotspot

Unlike the four on my driving side, the passenger seat on Priscilla offered only one, medium speed gear. Rusty panted his way up the first hill, staying quiet as he found his rhythm. It was great having company on the Bikecar and we chatted about everything from politics to owning a holiday cabin in the middle of Mississippi. Rusty was passionate about his business and during an ice-cream break at a small out-of-town gas station he managed to persuade the woman behind the counter that her and her family needed a break next to Black Creek. As he handed over his card I tried to make sense of some strange, apparently jellied shapes in a jar full of pink liquid. 'Pig trotters,' the woman told me, deftly unscrewing the lid and picking out a dripping trotter with a pair of tongs.

'And what are these for, exactly?' I asked, needing to hear confirmation.

'They for eatin',' she said, looking at me like I'd just smashed a window.

'That's what I thought.'

'You should have one,' said Rusty, which made me dislike him a little bit.

'Oh no, that won't be necessary,' I growled, turning my attention to the woman, 'my doctor tells me I'll never be able to eat pig trotter, it'll bring me out in hives.'

'I feel sorry for you,' she said sympathetically.

'I think I'll survive, but thanks for showing us,' I smiled, quickly ushering Rusty outside into the heat.

A couple pulled up and asked about the Bikecar. 'I'll take this one,' said Rusty, leaving me to suck on an ice lolly and read a newspaper featuring a celebratory picture of a small boy – a champion hunter - holding a gun three times the size of his body. Two minutes later Rusty had educated the couple in the car about my journey, and had also persuaded them to take a holiday at Black Creek Cabin. It was a wonder that the place had been available last night, the rate this man was selling his wares.

A skinny, haggard old man strolled out of the woods and over the road towards the rest stop. A cut off sleeve dangled emptily from his left shoulder. '*Alligator hunter,*' whispered Rusty.

'Are you serious?' I whispered back?

'Deadly,' he said.

'Can't be very good at it,' I pondered, as the man and his stump scuffled past us without returning our nods. A minute later he retraced his tracks, clutching two packets of ramen noodles in his remaining hand.

'That's the problem with the American system,' said Rusty, so many people living under the poverty line without help from the government. Shit, I lived off ramen noodles when I was a student, they're about the only food poor people can afford.'

We pedalled another 15 miles before the Sweetwater Baptist Church offered a decent camping spot. Rusty and I chatted for an hour before his wife and eldest son Ro picked him up, then I made a den beneath a picnic shelter's long concrete bench, draping my mosquito net either side to keep insects out.

I was brought out of sleep at 5am by the roar of a lawn mower. Peeking out of my hidey hole I spotted a lone gardener tending the grounds of the cemetery behind the church. Some more snooze would have been nice but it seemed an unlikely possibility, so I crawled to an upright position much like a sped up version of those primate-to-human evolution illustrations, then packed up the Bikecar quickly, still unsure whether I was actually allowed to have camped there. Just before I had time to get away the gardener approached me, thankfully with a big smile on his face. 'What are you doing?' he asked curiously.

'I'm riding to Miami!' I replied.

'On that?'

'Yes, her name's Priscilla,' I said, as though that would explain things.

'Ah,' he pondered, 'my daughter's name is Priscilla. Have a nice day.' And with that, the man walked slowly back to his mower, started it up and continued with his chores. *Perhaps he's just not fond of his daughter*, was the only reason I could think of for the abrupt ending of our conversation.

Just minutes into my day on the road I could have done without a woman shaking her arm at me as she drove past, shouting, 'Get ooofff the road. Go back to your own country, you're not welcome here!' I was confused as how she knew I was foreign; although perhaps it was obvious, me exercising and all.

Mississippi mornings in May are a treasure, the perfect 21 degree temperature offering an ideal foil for strenuous exercise. As with every morning so far, mist rose from the valley floor. Soft moisture permeated out of the delta surrounding the Pascagoula River, which had just claimed independence from the unification upstream of the Chickasawhay and the Leaf. I must have been enjoying myself because I was content to keep riding despite the temptation of finding a canoe and paddling the Pascagoula down to the Gulf.

Priscilla and I were finding our groove out there in the middle of the red States, dropping into gas stations and fielding amazed questions from gap toothed locals, who had never heard an English accent let alone considered a regime of such physical strain that my journey evidently required. I felt a sense of deep pleasure that this simple journey would instill such wonder, sometimes to the degree that an explanation of my intent to a local would result in a simple whistle, a resigned and confused release of air that revealed everything without a word.

I was chowing down on a disgusting yet delicious egg and bacon roll in one such roadside station when a grey-haired man pulled himself out of a battered old Chevy and gave me a friendly wave, with his *only* arm. *Another one-armed man?* He entered the store and by the time he came back outside and was passing the bench upon which I was seated I'd summoned the courage to speak to him. 'Say, Sir, what happened to your arm?'

He stopped and slowly turned a thin, tanned and stubbled face in my direction. 'Gator,' he said, 'big one.'

'Man, I'm sorry,' I gurgled.

'That's what you get when you play with teeth,' he said, tipping his hat in salute.

I made my way onto a six-lane highway which was so quiet it made the 10 foot wide shoulder – *my lane* – practically insignificant. Finally, after days of punishing climbs I was now approaching the coast and here was my reward, endless downhill runs infecting me with joy, uncontrollable screams of 'Yeeeeow!' as my cheeks became battered with rushing wind that whipped the breath out of my lungs. I ruddy loved those big falls, Priscilla held her line so well I never felt in danger of losing control despite her entire frame shaking considerably, and this plus the rare speed at which I was covering ground had me singing endlessly at the top of my voice.

Ah, the true exhilaration of slow travel drew the essence of life to the surface. Every leg-aching incline and the crash and the nighttime mosquitos and the proximity of cars and fumes were all worth it for this, for feeling alive, for living!

Thunderstorms had threatened all day but despite lightning thrashing the horizon I didn't feel a drop of rain until late afternoon. I sheltered beneath a mall overhang in the Mississippi town of Hurley, where several small frogs decided to jump all over Priscilla. I named one of them Fred and he stayed with me for at least ten minutes. The inclement weather continued and I decided to do the same, steering a little further from the roadside verge so as not to collide with one of several large snakes that had been brought out of the gutters by the rain.

Mississippi was almost behind me as I wound through the affluent suburbs 10 miles west of Mobile, wondering what I'd experience in Alabama. The answer may have been evident as I paused to stare at the green State Line sign, which was absolutely riddled with bullet holes. Twenty metres further on there was another sign, appearing to warn of tractors. This was going to be interesting.

Dusk fell swiftly and I found myself rattling down a dirt road having misinterpreted my phone's map. I was scanning every possible patch of grass and wooded area for a camping spot but perimeter fences and snake-friendly drainage ditches offered little potential. An American football landed on the road in front of me as I passed an enormous house with enough lawn around it to pitch 1,000 tents. A preppy-looking teenager and his mother came over to check out this sweaty and bearded ginger-haired man on a weird pedal car as he passed the ball back to them, and I felt sure they were going to offer me a place to camp, mainly because people are genuinely good at heart and in answer to their 'where are you going to sleep?' question I'd responded with,

'I'm not sure yet, I'm just looking for a place to camp.' Instead they said, 'we can't think of anywhere nearby, but there's a church ten miles south of here,' and then they walked across their grounds and shut the door. Teases!

With only about half an hour of light remaining I eventually settled on a patch of gravel at the entrance to a long driveway that led to an enormous house. A chain was slung across the path between two trees and a For Sale sign strongly informed me that progress beyond the chain was out of bounds and would be considered as trespassing. Although the main road was only a few metres away I figured that prospective buyers wouldn't be viewing property late on a Saturday night. I slung my Sky Tent between Priscilla and the sign right in the middle of the driveway, then crawled inside and thanked Paul Everitt for leaving a sleeping mat inside the Bikecar's old storage box, because without it I would have been rather uncomfortable.

*   *   *

'How fast will it run?'

'About ten miles an hour.'

'Eeeeeeee, maaaaan. Are you peddlin' or does it run off a motor?'

'Are you kiddin'?'

The Minute Mart in Green Bay, Alabama was a hive of activity for Sunday morning traffic. I'd been perched on Priscilla's passenger seat for half an hour and at least three people had gone into the store. I'm a coffee fiend, it's an addiction and I'm proud of it. I dream of coffee when I'm on the road, my creamy brown incentive to pedal harder and earn a rest stop. Americans love their coffee, which is why we get on so well. Every service station has a coffee corner or a coffee shelf or a coffee table, with a phenomenal variety of coffees on offer. Even in the middle of nowhere there are five choices of coffee for all the people who will never come in to try them. I love America, it provides service to all. I had balanced a coffee on Priscilla's chassis and was prying my way into a tin of pineapple with my penknife when he pulled up: an old guy with a short afro who seemed so infinitely drunk that he could barely get out of his truck. He wobbled towards me with an empty pint glass in his hand: an old tankard with a handle like you'd find in an English country pub. 'What have you got in your glass there?' I asked, pointing,

'Oh, that,' he slurred, hanging his head, 'I'm just gonna get some coffee…'

A woman smiled at us as she left the store, 'what it that?' she asked, looking at Priscilla.

'That's cool ain't it?' said the drunk guy,

'Ahhh that's somin' else,' laughed the women, and then she looked at me, 'Where'd y'all come from?'

'From England. London, England, and I'm heading to Miami.'

'Oh wow, good for you baybee!'

I bid my new friends farewell, but not before the man had fallen flat on his face when entering the shop, smashing his glass all over the floor. 'Yup, I need me some coffee,' he confirmed, brushing dust from his pants.

Off I rode towards the sea, the land now totally flat and

prepared for the coast. I pedalled nervously down a road called Defender's Way and past a Gun Port, which seemed to be a place where people went to shoot pieces of paper with human silhouettes on. Afterwards, they'd probably buy sniper rifles to protect their homes with. They do like their weapons in America, especially in the South. Guns are very much part of the fabric of the United States and firearm homicides are sadly accepted as part of life, an apparently worthwhile compromise for homeowners to feel safe on their own property.

As a born and bred Englishman I know that it's possible to feel safe in your own home *without* owning a gun, but also hear the argument that as guns are so dominant in the States that any attempt to cut down on ownership would be futile, leaving people open to attack without being able to defend themselves. All this said, it's the supposition that humans *will* attack other humans that worries me. More than four times as many people are killed with guns in the USA each year than in any other developed country in the world, but the USA is also very close to the top of the charts in non-firearm homicides, as well.

I don't have the answers for why American society seems to breed and even glorify violence, but arguments for video games and Hollywood gore and even a history of violence don't explain much lower rates of gun crime in other parts of the world, where games and films are just as accessible, and wars have raged throughout history. I've had the 'gun discussion' countless times and have grown familiar with 'guns don't kill people, people kill people.' All I know is, people *plus* guns kill people very easily, and if everybody is allowed a gun there's more likelihood for the end of the most sacred thing human beings have: life.

Take into account politics and religion and socio-economic variance and western culture as much as you like but the only dominant factors that separate the United States from the rest of the world are the widespread availability of guns and the fact that Americans have half as much holiday as any other nation enjoying a western society. Hell, the USA is the *only* high capita country where employers are not required by law to provide a single day of paid leave. Research shows that of the two weeks holiday Americans are allowed some are afraid to take it for fear of losing their jobs. Perhaps everyone's just tired and overworked here? Perhaps they need an adventure?

I pedalled fast after thinking about all of that, fully prepared to jump into survival mode at the faintest threat. Almost instantly a red car swept up alongside me and stopped, right in the middle of the road. 'What ya doin'?' shouted a man in a deeply southern accent. There were two men in the car, one of those cheap models that is a bit low to the ground and could easily be mistaken for a Porsche if you had, say, cataracts. As I said, I was already primed to defend myself against attack and stealthily readied my best weapon, my GoPro. Camera now pointed towards my foe I engaged them,

'I'm heading to Miami!'

'On that thing?!'

'No no, on a unicycle, but I just thought I'd take this four-wheel bicycle for a spin, you know how it is.'

I don't want you to think that I was antagonising these chaps, it's just that I have a horrible habit of behaving like a pompous idiot when in the company of rednecks. It's just a harmless game; I like to see when they actually listen to me instead of picking their gums. They didn't seem to have found a problem with my unicycle story and continued their line of questioning. 'Did you make that?

I considered being truthful but the story seemed too long-winded, so I said,

'Yes, it took a couple of days but everything seems to be okay.'

'And you're pedalling that thing?'

'It would appear so. I wanted to put a motor on it but I hear that there will be no gas left in America by the end of next week.' They looked at each other in horror, one of them spat on the ground.

'You wanna come to our place? You can stay the night if you like.'

'Umm, it's okay, it's only 10am and I've got about eight hundred miles to cycle so I better be moving along.'

'No really, we've got a great yard, are you camping?'

They were becoming unsettlingly insistent. 'It's very nice of you,' I said, 'but it takes a while to get around on this thing. Plus, I need to be fetching my unicycle.'

They seemed to be getting bored, because the next step was something I'd grown familiar with during my American travels. I'd shared a tiny morsel of information about my own journey because they'd asked, and now it was their turn to tell me everything about everyone they'd ever met.

Several cars screeched past, beeping their horns at this idiot red vehicle stationary in the middle of the road, but the men didn't notice and once the passenger had told me about a pig he once killed with a pistol the driver shared a lovely tale about a man he knew who once drove a car around the entire circumference of Florida. The kid nearest to me threw a cigarette butt out of the window onto the floor then stared hard at my camera, 'you filmin'?' he asked, scowling.

'Yep,' I said. He seemed taken aback with my honesty,

199

perhaps he wasn't used to it. He coughed a little. 'You have to watch that smoking,' I said earnestly, 'it'll kill ya.'

There was silence. For too long to be comfortable.

'Right then,' I chirped brightly, 'lovely to meet you gentleman, you have a nice drive.'

'We might see you later,' said the driver,

'You never know,' I said, starting to move the pedals and for the first time in the entire journey wishing that the Bikecar had a touch of acceleration.

A new word had formed in my mind, a term that forever more would be used to describe the behaviour of men like this; men who would never contribute to society, men who laugh in the face of traffic safety, men who litter, men who hunt alligators and sometimes lose an arm. *Redneckability*: it has a ring to it, don't you think?

I reached the sea and took a moment to reflect. The first and last time I'd seen the Gulf of Mexico was eight months previous and 100 miles further towards the south west. That day in early September 2011 will always stay with me. My friend John Ruskey joined me for the beautiful, peaceful final miles of my three-month paddle. Culminating out beyond mild breakers, the southernmost outlet of the Mississippi River yawned in pleasure at having spat me out. All of those months of planning followed by more months of non-stop movement, experiences, sights, sounds, friends and challenges, all coming to a stop in open water. A flash of memories washed away with a final, exultant leap from my paddleboard into the Gulf. Salt water: a brief reward for such a time of fresh adventure.

And here was the ocean again all around me as I pedalled the early stretches of a two-mile causeway across to Dauphin Island, the Gulf sparkling blue on either side. I've always been calmed by water but its meditative qualities were tested by eager, speeding weekenders. The shoulder was slight and all of a sudden the island-bound traffic increased in density, some of the vehicles taking umbrage at my presence with sharp, stabbing horns. Wide trailers followed most of the trucks, boats riddled with lines and floating toys all prepared for a Sunday afternoon fishing trip.

I spent half the time on the verge, waiting for a gap in the cars before pedalling furiously until the next batch of vehicles approached. Then I was forced to rest once more. Eventually I reached a nemesis that had taunted me for the best part of an hour, a horrendously steep bridge that rose swiftly from the causeway, thankfully with a Bikecar-wide shoulder. As with all hills I gave it my best shot in the early stages, upping the gears and using inertia until it couldn't survive against the incline, and then I had to get off and push.

Vehicles sped by just inches from my back and I had to keep my finger as tight on the brakes as my nerve, one slip and Priscilla would roll out of my grasp in an instant, such was the gradient. Another obstacle I had to stay cautious about was glass on the roads. Whether I was pedalling or pushing I was keen to avoid a puncture delay, both for the time it would take and the test it would give to my patience and mending skills. The shoulder on the Dauphin Island bridge was a resting ground for litter and glass and I couldn't always avoid rolling over it. The rise brought me little excitement and I was overjoyed at reaching the top; taking a moment to enjoy the view, the fishing boats below, a small pod of dolphins frolicking.

What goes up must come down, but the joy of gratuitously taking advantage of gravity when plummeting downhill on a narrow shoulder is dampened a little by caution. I imagined the worst: Priscilla striking an overly large piece of roadside debris or a wheel coming off and sending me out into the road in time for a collision that would result in the Bikecar and me sailing over the protective wall into the water far below.

I applied the brakes regularly, firmly focused on keeping a straight line, then whooped with joy when the road levelled out so gradually that I barely had to pedal for the final 800 metres to the island. And as soon as I reached dry land again two people stood at the roadside beside their vehicle, cheering and clapping and generally acting like they knew exactly what I was doing. So it was with great surprise that when I came close enough to see their faces I realised that they had taken part in the Bluz Cruz race at Vicksburg. 'We were driving over here for a day on the beach and when we saw you we realised who it was!' smiled Dana.

'Can we buy you an ice cream? It's a hot one today,' offered Nick.

'I will never turn down an ice cream in these conditions,' I chuckled, 'so good to see you guys, how random!'

Half an hour later we'd bade goodbye and I was parking Priscilla in a queue for the ferry across the water to Fort Morgan, a short hop across the water to the other side of Mobile Bay.

Pedestrians and drivers stared at me in disbelief as the gates opened and I *pedalled* up the ramp and stopped between chalk markings on the deck as though I was a normal vehicle. The ferry attendants didn't know what to make of me, 'I guess you don't have a motor?' the ticket inspector asked,

'No Sir, all legs!'

'How far you riding?'

'To Miami from Memphis.'

'Oh my goodness.'

*　　*　　*

The ferry ride was a pleasant break despite the omnipresence of oil derricks across Mobile Bay and further out into the Gulf. I tried to imagine how this bay scene had been before humans were ever here but the roar of the ferry engine and a constant need to check that Priscilla wasn't about to roll with the movement of the boat stopped me dreaming. I'd developed an ingenious technique to stop Priscilla rolling on a slope, in the absence of a handbrake a short bungee rope wrapped around the brake and handlebar then clipped into my water bottle holder kept my girl still. She may have been drawing concerned glances from all around but I was proud of her, we'd already ridden close to 250 miles and would forever have indelible memories together.

'Have a good one brother,' the attendant said with one hand raised towards me as I pedalled off the ferry.

Compared to the luscious gardens on Dauphin Island the Fort Morgan side of the bay was totally arid. It wasn't long before I passed the fort itself, apparently one of the finest examples of military architecture in the Western world, but I didn't stop. I've never been one for landmarks or attractions and besides, I once saw a fort a decade earlier and when you've seen a fort, you've seen a fort.

A thousand lonely beach huts, houses and mansions had amassed themselves on not much more than a desert spit. There was little movement in the area as I made my way along the only road that connected back with the mainland but I could only imagine the utter carnage of a busy holiday weekend in this part of the world. The Gulf Coast was a mecca for Southerners and I expected a busy week slowly moving through the urban conurbations that tend to line any coastline in the developed world.

I dodged a couple of snakes that were commuting across the road and became quickly tired by a dry and forceful easterly wind that sometimes gusted so hard it brought me straight to a standstill. I'd decided to skip lunch in order to catch the ferry so opted for an early dinner in order to prevent my stomach from eating itself. I pulled into the car park of a quiet little Mexican restaurant, took off most of my clothes and hung them on the handlebars to dry; suffice to say that riding a ¼ tonne quad is wet work. I redressed, pulled my hammock from the storage box and draped it over Priscilla's seats, it was still damp from the morning dew. Inside I ordered the cheapest thing on the menu and surreptitiously plugged all of my electronics in to charge.

'What are you doing here?' asked a blonde lady a few tables away upon hearing my accent. She was the only one in the place apart from me and a family of five Mexicans who crowded around a plasma screen, watching music videos.

'I'm riding to Miami on that thing outside,' I smiled. She was beautiful, about 50 years old, with eyes that had almost certainly melted a few hearts in their time. She introduced herself as Terri, listened to my story and then said,

'My daughter would kill me if she heard me saying this, but if you don't have anywhere to stay tonight you're welcome to a spare room at my place. There's a storm coming.'

'That's really kind of you, I had no idea there was bad weather on the way. Are you sure?'

'Well, you look like a nice guy, although....are you a nice guy?'

'I am! Honestly! But I completely understand if you want to withdraw your offer. Hey, here's my card, get your daughter to check my website if you like!'

I returned to my table and a few minutes later the lady came over again, this time ready to leave. 'I trust you,' she said, 'my place is about ten miles further up the road, would you like a lift?'

'Oh no, I'll start riding very soon and will be there in about an hour and a half, is that okay?'

'That's perfect, here's my address, but be quick, the storm is starting. '

She wasn't wrong, my gear had been blown all over the parking lot. I collected it from fence posts, a tree, the flowerbed that bordered the restaurant, and then I spotted a pair of my boxer shorts hanging on a wing mirror just as the owner, another woman, approached the car in question. She seemed perturbed. Then began the long ride to Terri's house. It might seem like a strange situation, a young male traveller taking refuge with a female stranger, but I trusted my gut and she had taken a leap of faith and trusted hers. She'd been lovely and cautious, but her goodwill had won a battle over the demons of societal expectation, which would have been whispering into her ear '*are you mad?!*'

Darkness welcomed the rain just as I reached the house, a gorgeous little bungalow separated from the bay side of the spit by just fifty metres of grass and sand. A small dog yapped around my ankles and that's about the only complaint I could have about my stay with Terri in Gulf Shores, Alabama. My host was sweet, open and kind and we chatted late into the night. Strangers are just friends waiting to happen, and Terri Johnson was proof of the pudding.

19

Playing Chicken

'Wait!' Terri said urgently before rushing back into her house and returning with a small cool box. 'I never use this anymore, it'd be good for you to keep things cold, I put some ice in there, too.' I hugged her tightly, said my thanks and pedalled up the drive away from her house. I could see her in my wing mirror stood stock still, watching this strange man leave her life just as quickly as he'd arrived. I raised one hand in the air, a final wave before I disappeared.

It was a calm, cool morning with traces of moisture in the air and I made a decent dash through the tourist trap of Gulf Shores before rush hour traffic became too heavy. I work on a system of self reward, only allowing a break once it has been earned. My GPS clocked a fraction over 12 miles by the time I passed a Waffle House on the outskirts of town, a good enough chunk to warrant some eggs and bacon. Under the watchful eye of the morning clientele I pulled into the sloping lot, placed my helmet behind the back wheel as a chock and just for safe measure, wrapped the handbrake bungee into place.

It was a picture of happiness in my own mind; many miles travelled, in the middle of a wonderful journey full of ups and downs, and of course I was sitting at a kiosk with a knife in one hand and fork in the other being presented with a breakfast platter so big a professional wrestler would have baulked. The waitress looked at me and saw a bearded man with scruffy red hair in a royal blue t-shirt with the sleeves cut off. The back of the shirt drenched in sweat, a mouth so hungry the teeth were out, a vehicle on the other side of the window that clearly wouldn't be driven by a sane person. She grunted when I said 'Good morning,' practically threw the food at me and strutted away with her chin held high. 'Thank you!' I called after her, meaning it from the bottom of my heart. Not only had she served me a delicious pile of eggs and meat, but she'd saved me parting with a healthy tip, too!

Belly full I pedalled on, reeling in Parasol West and then Perdido Beach, where I paused briefly beside a sign that informed me that the road behind belonged to Alabama, and the road ahead to Florida. Although I was still less than a third of the distance between Memphis and Miami so much had happened already that I couldn't help feeling sad at this indicator of progress. I was into my last State of the journey already, exactly one week after saying goodbye to Tim and Wayne at Crystal Springs. What would 700 miles of the Sunshine State have in store for me?

Temptation, I decided, was not one of the things Florida would tease me with, as I pedalled easily past the Waffle House which guarded the State line all seductive with its yellow frontage and big steaks. This coastline was tourism central, prime real estate for holiday homes and businesses praying on the disposable bucks of the masses. Every shop sold inflatables, trinkets, and postcards, items that would be purchased for a week's use then discarded or hidden in a cupboard somewhere. Every block there was a fleet of colourful battery-driven buggies, go-carts or novelty bicycles, all ready for hire and photo opportunities. Thou shalt not *walk* in America, they screamed.

Much like the Florida east coast the Gulf Coast is twofold, the mainland often separated from the ocean by a narrow lagoon or sound, and then an island, or key. Looking ahead, I saw that my enjoyable – if not cultural – route along these thin slices of land would soon be broken by an unabridged span of water offering access into the various bays surrounding the city of Pensacola, so a forced course inland was necessary.

Bridges were becoming my nemesis. Even on the busiest of highways and the narrowest of shoulders I was always afforded a little comfort by some kind of roadside verge, which I could rely on in case I needed to swiftly evade a runaway vehicle. On bridges, however, limited space meant there was no such escape. The provision of a shoulder was hit or miss and in the absence of one I still had no choice but to pedal like crazy until I got to the other side. When a bridge came into my sights I prayed for a shoulder, which offered both safety and a relief of the stress caused by the Bikecar having to actively block an entire lane and hold up – and therefore antagonise – traffic.

Had I been charting my blood pressure on these journeys the highest spikes would have represented long bridges, with no shoulders, at rush hour. It took about three hours, four bridges and 15 miles of navigating suburban roads between leaving Perdido Key and my approach to what would turn out to be one of the journey's most intense challenges. Pensacola's Bay Bridge, also known as Three Mile Bridge, was nothing but a low concrete drag with a small humped bridge in the centre to allow for water traffic, but as the only direct link between Pensacola and Gulf Breeze, Florida, the two lanes in each direction are always kept busy. By the time I reached the bridge darkness was falling fast and I felt there was little choice but to make the crossing and get out of the city.

There was nowhere for me to sleep safely there.

I dug out every torch and flashlight I had and taped them all to the back of the storage box and up my flagpoles. Priscilla looked like a Christmas tree once the job was done and I took off onto the bridge, thankful for my increased visibility and the provision of a shoulder that was the exact width of the Bikecar. Of course, this left absolutely no margin for error. Cars and trucks flashed by just inches to my left and the morbid nightmares I'd had on the bridge to Dauphin Island seemed so much more likely to come true here, one slight misjudgement by myself or another vehicle and I'd either be crushed against the sidewall or flung into the water. But I was committed and all I could do was stick as close to the wall as possible and not let my left wheels cross the white line. I hoped – almost desperately - that the concentration I had to maintain for this three mile stretch was shared by all the other drivers on the bridge that night.

The traffic was end to end and as the darkness increased the hallucinogenic scene of tail and headlights blurring into the blackness gave me a strange, peaceful resignation. I was travelling my way, so close and in the same direction as all of these cars, but our purposes couldn't have been more different. They may have been travelling ten times as fast as me but I would eventually go further and experience more than many of them, in my own time and at my own pace.

It took 45 minutes to reach the southern end of the bridge but I saw to my horror that just as the bridge reached land the shoulder disappeared and it was at least two hundred metres to the next junction. Of course, the density and speed of the motorised traffic didn't change just because the shoulder disappeared and without thinking twice I turned off the road, thrust my legs hard down onto the pedals and powered my way up a grass verge and over the other side, crashing down a steep slope and straight into a near empty parking lot. Less than ten seconds after leaving the highway I was parked and still; panting, leaking with sweat, the intensity of the crossing rivaled and made worthwhile by the gorgeous off-roading at the end.

I stared out at the water and the bridge over which I'd come, and laughed out loud. Then, feeling eyes on me, I looked to my left and saw a man and a woman coming towards me, walking away from what I presumed was their pickup, which was covered in splattered paint and had two Stand Up Paddleboards sticking out of it.

Bruce and Lisa were angels to me that evening. They'd been out scouting for a possible evening paddle but had just decided against it when I arrived, bouncing into the car park. They couldn't believe that I'd just crossed the bridge, let alone pedalled my contraption from central Mississippi, and took a few moments to think about my request for somewhere to camp that night. They told me they lived back in Pensacola town and that I was welcome to join them, but the absence of a place to store the Bikecar securely put paid to that. Instead, Bruce had a brainwave, called a friend and got permission for me to camp at a house on the next island over. 'We're not exactly sure where it is, but we'll find it,' he said, beaming. 'We'll shadow you in the truck to protect you from traffic, all you need to do is go straight, cross the next bridge and then it's a straight shot down the key.'

'Just so you know, the last time someone drove behind me they got hit by another car,' I warned, but it didn't seem to put them off.

We set off, Bruce and Lisa in the truck with all their lights flashing, and in two miles sure enough another bridge loomed. During my last look at the map I'd been so focused on Three Mile Bridge that I hadn't considered my next route, so this nighttime voyage was wreaking havoc with my bearings. I had no idea where the bridge would take me, it was much steeper than the previous one and before I knew it Lisa was jumping into the passenger seat beside me and lending her legs to the effort.

She pedalled seven miles with me that night as Bruce faithfully kept guard to the rear, and before we knew it Bruce was shouting to turn left and we'd made our destination. All the houses in the neighbourhood were up on stilts with parking bays underneath, and pointing at a big white house Bruce told me I was welcome to camp in the underbelly. There was an open shower in the corner and a hammock already swinging between two supporting beams; it was utterly perfect. We hugged, they wished me luck then drove away, and I counted my lucky blessings. I'd been ready for bed two hours earlier and meeting these two had not only found me a delightful place to rest, but had put ten more miles on the clock. With Lisa's help I'd pedalled 55 miles that day, the longest yet by some distance, and I felt it. I drifted off in the hammock in seconds, dreaming of blurry, speeding lights on bridges.

*   *   *

I couldn't believe the scene I woke up to. The Santa Rosa Sound was mirror calm, the only ripples caused by jumping fish. I'd known there was water nearby all night but didn't expect it to be just ten metres from my hammock, what a gorgeous treat! I took my time packing up, showering in a make-shift wooden cubicle, texting Bruce and Lisa a huge thank you.

Priscilla reversed down the sloping drive with a bump and then we made our way forwards, out of the beach estate and left onto Gulf Boulevard. The next two hours was a treat, Santa Rosa island was less than 300 metres wide and off to my right the Gulf spread away into the distance. A pod of five dolphins tracked me for ten miles, travelling at exactly my pace, even stopping and playing around when I pulled over to make some film and take photos. It was hard not to feel happy discovering such a place and the only sadness was that I couldn't share it with anyone. I desperately wanted Em by my side that day.

A single road ran down the centre of the key with sand and dunes either side and not a building in sight until I reached the settlement of Navarre. Here I faced a frustrating detour. The island continued eastwards but a disused Air Force base, a former missile testing site, lay in between Navarre and Destin, which lay across the bridge from the end of the island. Had I been on a lighter contraption I might have tried to stealth my way through the base in order to avoid yet another bridge crossing and an undoubtedly busy afternoon of traffic heading into the city of Fort Walton, but Priscilla was not the craft for stealth. I fought over the bridge, took a right and faced the worst three hours of the entire journey. Damn Air Force bases.

As good as the morning had been the afternoon was about to put my good nature to the test and reverse my fortunes, I was faced with a raging, disgusting highway with two feet of shoulder for 5' 7" of Bikecar. Try as I might to avoid busy roads sometimes there is just no alternative. America is built for driving, for automobiles, for guzzling gas; it can be merciless for a self-powered traveller. I was always going to run into the occasional difficulty having chosen to ride such a wide pedal car and it was all a part of the adventure, but as the hours drew on the line between acceptable hardship and unacceptable danger became increasingly thinner.

For fifteen miles I crunched over a white gravel and chalk verge, my left wheels – connected directly to the drive chain - just touching the very edge of the concrete road in order to gain purchase. Every four minutes brief respite appeared thanks to the last set of traffic lights which held traffic up, each time I had maybe ten or twenty seconds of empty road that I turned onto and plundered furiously, gaining so much more ground than my careful, grinding progress on the glass and nail-riddled verge but still only a few preciously stolen metres at a time.

I was doing everything I could to continue moving forwards at the same time as staying alive. I took no undue risks but several times cars veered off their lane that afternoon, the hot air of their proximity blasting my skin and my heart, debris showering the Bikecar. So often there was a clear lack of concentration of the drivers alongside, exacerbated by an innately local attitude of driving right up the rear of the car in front, leaving no decent time to brake or correct in case of emergency. I estimated that over 70,000 vehicles passed me in those 10 miles and 4 and a half hours, an eternity of blowing horns and single fingers and double fingers and the whizz whoosh whap of vehicles rushing by.

I was a tired and weary man by the time I found myself in Fort Walton. No adventure was worth the danger I'd just experienced. I had learned, gained or benefitted not one bit from the close calls dished out by Highway 98 that day, and after an hour's rest to calm down, regain strength and refuel I looked at the map and saw the same road stretching on for miles and decided to do something that I'd never previously considered. I made the call to skip a section, to break the linear integrity of the journey in place of preserving my safety. There is no honour in dying unnecessarily at a roadside, I had no need for another life-preserving crunch of dry vegetation as I swerved right to relative calm, my threshold for safety vs purity had been reached, so I leapt into the unknown.

On a bicycle I'd have taken it on and made greater progress with less risk, but the Bikecar's girth was asking for trouble in a part of the world where everyone moving somewhere else is forced onto the same road. Respect for cyclists is already minimal; respect for Bikecar riders doesn't come into it. Already in 340 miles I'd counted over 200 roadside memorials and I wasn't ready to be recognised by a wooden cross.

The final straw had been the bridge stretching over the Sound to Okaloosa Island. No shoulder, three lanes of end-to-end traffic, my white flag. I asked the police if they could shepherd me across, they said no. I had no right to their time or resources but wanted to exhaust my options. The bridge carried the 98 and locals told me the road had a tendency towards accidents. My interest in gaining a similar reputation was zero, I'd had my quota for this trip. I phoned a friend. I made a call. I put my life jacket on and took Priscilla off the road for a stretch. Leslie Kolovich, a radio presenter who I'd spoken to multiple times over the phone about my adventures but had never met in person, lived 30 miles east. She sourced a trailer and along with her friend Joan, a local photographer, drove to Fort Walton to pluck me off the road. I gazed out at the highway as we drove, discerning how I felt about not being out there on the tarmac. I felt nothing. I was glad not to be there. It was a ruthless section surrounded by fast food joints and shopping malls. This was no place for a man without a motor.

The next morning I woke and grappled for a few minutes about creating a gap in my dotted line. Then a spontaneous Skype call with my friend Sarah who was still in Japan, waiting patiently for a weather window so she could begin her rowing voyage across the Pacific. I didn't tell her about my previous day's dilemma but without prompting she said, 'I've been talking with my friends here about making decisions, and when it isn't fun you know what the right decision is.' Sarah was one of the few people I knew in the adventure community who did what she did primarily for the fun factor. She was a unique soul, eternally positive, capable of achieving great things with a smile. Her words rang true, yep, my challenge had lost its fun for a while there. I wasn't chasing a record, I was riding to meet people, for the challenge, to see a cross section of a place I knew little about. I had no desire for near misses, they were not the type of story I wanted to share. A gap in the line meant I raised my chances of reaching the end of it in one piece. There was no dilemma, no lingering doubt, I'd made the correct decision.

There would be similar decisions in the future and I'd take each one on its merit. The Bikecar has its own beauty, Priscilla is my home right now but by God she's a wide, heavy bitch. I will take her out into the open road with empty country on one side and Gulf on the other and barely any other metal tankers to share the experience with and we will be right as rain once more. Another lesson learned. I am here to live, and one cannot be a chicken if they wish to avoid playing chicken.

20

Around the Point

If there was to be any negative karma as a result of moving forwards a short step with fuel, it appeared in the form of Leslie's two tiny dogs, Skip and Buddy, who lurked around my feet for a day but were thankfully quiet. Despite the presence of my tiny, furry nemeses I felt strangely at home. Leslie's soothing radio voice was so familiar to me after our interviews and I sent a message home to please my Mum, who had often mentioned 'that lady on the radio with the lovely voice, oh it's gorgeous!'

The previous day's efforts had left me exhausted so I stayed a full day with the Kolovich's, heading into the picturesque town of Seaside, where Jim Carrey's The Truman Show was filmed and Leslie had her studio in the local school. We chatted on air for half an hour about life choices and adventure, and were joined by Leslie's daughters Maddie and Olivia, who were nearing that terrifying age where young humans have to try and decide what to do for the rest of their lives with barely any life experience to base their choices on.

That evening a few of Leslie's friends came around for a delicious meal, including Gabriel Grey, a former bull rider who loved his Stand Up Paddleboarding. We chatted adventure and gear all night. Gabe was preparing to join another Florida-based paddler by the name of Justin Riney on a few warm-up paddles, in preparation for Justin taking off around the entire Florida coastline the following year. I got out my Sky Tent and showed Gabe how simple it was to set up both as a tent and a hammock - and my favourite bit of all, the 15-second pack-away time.

As good as it is to stop for a day and rest the old muscles, I was ready to get going the next morning. I breakfasted with the Kolovich's before they departed for work and school. The day was pleasant and I moved eastwards swiftly, enjoying several quiet 'old' roads that took me a short distance off the main highways but still arrowed parallel along the coast, just with fewer cars. There wasn't a great deal of traffic on the approach to Panama City but slowly the natural coastline became overcome by retirement villages, holiday resorts and gigantic shopping malls.

I have to admit, America does opulent, bright and crazy very well indeed. Why have a normal entrance to a swimwear shop when you can build an enormous shark on the front of the building and have customers walk in through the mouth? Why have a big novelty house when you can build it as though it's upside down? And why not have a theme park of some variety every other block? This was kid heaven, rollercoasters and arcades and mini golf and, should the need arise, an entire body of water covered in lilos, pedalos and jet skis. Then, once you need a good meal, less than three minutes on a golf cart, battery-powered mini sports car or Segway would have you at the entrance of a McDonalds, Dunkin' Donuts or Cheeseburger World.

It was utter paradise, mainly because everyone was having fun and nobody was driving. This all changed as I crossed the bridge into the city, taking advantage of an enormous hard shoulder until it disappeared and I was drafted automatically into one of three lanes of high speeding traffic. Just as comfort kills ambition a high degree of discomfort will prove to be incredibly motivating to your survival, and my legs did their best to allow Priscilla to imitate a Formula One car until I could escape over the verge into a parking lot, and safety. Sadly, one driver took umbrage at my existence and left the highway to come and find me in the parking lot, where he unloaded a great deal of obscenities and asked if I wanted a fight. It seemed like a strange way to settle a dispute so I opted on something better by pedalling down an alleyway that was a little too narrow for his enormous truck. Of course, he could have run after me if he truly wanted to play, but he was one of those men who only exercise with a short walk between the bar and the rest room so I fancied my chances. 'My car is faster than yours!' he shouted a final, well thought out assault through his window.

'You must be compensating for something!' I sung back, hoping the man wasn't intelligent enough to realise that all he needed to do was drive to the opposite side of the block to continue the conversation. He wasn't and he didn't.

The backstreets and suburbs of Panama City were surprisingly delightful. I weaved through a patchwork of roads beneath overhanging trees that scented the air like a restaurant on Valentine's night, then struck gold by finding a cycle path that took me the remaining ten miles across the city. One final goliath of a bridge, this one without a shoulder, and I was delivered out of town and into the countryside as though passing through a looking glass; as soon as you're on the other side there is no looking back.

I charged ahead, the decrease in traffic giving me the liberty to remain fully on the road, and then an odd thing happened. I stopped for a reason of nature and felt the wind tugging at my hair. Looking back towards Priscilla I saw the flags behind her frantically pointing forwards.

Forwards! I had a tail wind! I have travelled over 12,000 miles under my own steam in recent years and have only enjoyed about four hours of tailwind; it truly was a rare experience! A weight lifted; the difference was supreme, I sped along unblocked by the invisible wall of air that usually resisted my wide vehicle even with the most gentle of headwinds. Then, as has become customary in a life where I rarely choose the easy path, I made life hard for myself.

I spotted what was marked as a bicycle trail on my map running parallel to the highway a few hundred metres to my right. Rush hour was approaching and I couldn't help thinking that a cycle path *plus* a tailwind would be utopia, so I made my way up a dusty track towards where I thought the cycle path was, and found a rutted four-wheel trail partially overgrown with grass and covered in a thick layer of sand. *Ah well, this'll be fun, and it probably turns into a paved road at some point* I thought, and before I knew it I'd gone too far to turn back, despite the path becoming progressively more overgrown and Priscilla's wheels spinning in the loose sand every few seconds. A seven foot alligator trotted across the path, too fast and unexpected for me to catch the moment on camera. A mosquito bit me, then another. I consoled myself with an old Chinese saying that mosquitos are only attracted to the sexy people.

227

It was time to go back to the highway so I chose the next connecting path, which took me straight up to an orange metal barrier with a fence stretching out from it in either direction. Luckily Priscilla just about fit underneath the bar once I pushed down on the top of the office chair and limbo'd the flagpoles to horizontal, and once more, after two hours in a wood, I found myself on tarmac.

I slept in between the beach and the road just outside the peaceful, linear coastal town of Mexico Beach, arriving just in time to receive a $5 dollar donation from the local sheriff but just too late to get food from the nearest bar. Nutella and pita bread filled a hole. Up early with the sun and on the road by 7am, motivated to travel some distance before Friday afternoon traffic became dominant. Even the enormous bridge at Port St Joe didn't break my good mood, forged by 10 miles pedalled by breakfast, a welcome McDonalds coffee and three gorgeous, graceful manta rays that flapped and glided their way through shallow waters a stone's throw from the highway. I had Counting Crows in my ears and Walt Disney on my mind.

Em had been texting me from the Disney Institute at Orlando's Disney World, where she'd spent the week on an intensive Business Excellence course learning the Disney method of connecting inspired leadership to employee motivation. Initially I was confused why Em was going to Disney to learn about business but the information she fed back to me was bolstered by a clear indication that she was nothing but impressed by what she had experienced, both theoretically in the classroom and then through tours of all the Disney 'Kingdoms'.

The Walt Disney Empire has maintained its success for over 80 years through creativity, innovation, principles of engagement and, most of all, fun. It is said that 'Disney World is the happiest place on the Planet' and the key stemmed from the fact that the organisation hadn't shifted from its core values, which had been bred by Walt and his brother Roy. From what I could gather, Roy was the business brain and Walt the creative, the innovator, the one who placed happiness highest on his list of priorities. When Walt drew out the early plans for Disneyland he simply wanted to design a place where his employees could happily spend time with their children, saying, 'I want it to look like nothing else in the world. And it should be surrounded by a train.'

Walt Disney always had his head in the future. Disney World, the place where Em was texting me from, was born from Disney's original EPCOT concept, or Experimental Prototype City of Tomorrow, which he saw as a 'community of the future,' a place which would constantly innovate new systems and materials to benefit the wider world. Sadly, Walt's death meant most of his plans were abandoned, but the crux behind his mindset lived on in all of Disney's practices and I had one thing to thank him for, his choice of site meant that Em was now nearer to Northern Florida than Southern, which made it rather convenient for her to come and visit me once her course finished that weekend. All I had to do, of course, was pedal Priscilla 150 miles in 3 days to our designated meeting spot in Perry, Florida.

I pedalled hard around the Apalachicola Peninsula, remaining vigilant despite the usual emptiness of the roads. I have learned the bizarre failings in highway common sense by studying patterns on the road, so gut-wrenchingly frequent. Sometimes ten minutes would pass without a car and then wham, ten to twenty vehicles would career past at high speed in a tight convoy. I deplore what I have nicknamed 'The Metallic Conga of Death,' exhibiting an infuriating custom so regular in the South where cars would tailgate just inches behind the one in front, however high the speed at which they travelled. It would take just one of them to brake, adjust or defer from a consistent speed and there would be a multi-car pile-up, swerving cars bringing people in other lanes into danger.

On two occasions I found myself staring right down

the grill of a car that had pulled out of a speeding convoy, blind to anything in the opposite lane. As soon as they leave the line their space closes out so the only option was for me, or it, to leave the road. I made the decision both times, swerving off the road to the tune of screeching brakes from my opponent, just seconds from a head on collision. It's exhausting, to say the least, having the validity of your life questioned by stupidity. The lack of respect for all other drivers - whether motorised or non-motorised - in this country is astonishing but not surprising. After all, statistics tell me that I've been travelling through country that is home to the most obese and unfit people in the world. If people don't ride then they don't know what it feels like to be a rider.

This lifestyle is encouraged by culture. The idea of riding anything but an enormous truck around the corner to the fast food eatery is laughed out of town down here by 90% of the population. Of course, the lack of sidewalks or cycle paths means society gently encourages folk to sit upon a motor for even the shortest of journeys, deflating any understanding what those lithe, exercising people are doing down there on the road with their pedals. Because of this America has guzzled up three of my nine lives on this journey, and with that estimation I'm being generous. My internal fury was raised each time the conga thrashed past, along with the humbling sight of so many roadside memorials, crosses, wreaths and signs reading *Drive Safely*, *RIP Robbie*, *Speed Kills* or *Too Young to Die*. So many lives senselessly cut short, and for what? To get somewhere fast?

Of over 200 motorcycles that passed me in that opening fortnight only a handful wore helmets. 'We have a right not to,' say the unprotected. At some point, the wind in the hair might cost some of them their functions, if not their lives. My God, it's like everyone has a death wish. But of course if people can't understand the intricacies of their own mortality I shouldn't expect them to care about mine, so I remain tied to a personal policy that I should act like I'm invisible. Not two seconds passed without a glance to the wing mirror to assess the ever-approaching danger of cars, motorcycles, log trucks and other vehicles.

Priscilla's width means I rarely fit entirely within a roadside shoulder and my life is dependent on an ability to get out of the way when another driver isn't paying attention. I mustn't assume I've been seen by anyone and therefore if there's the slightest chance that I could be struck I move off the road. Sadly, this is often. It has been slow going but I'm still here, still breathing, still enjoying the challenge, still learning. My average day sees me moving for 7 hours and stopped for three and a half. That is how long I spend in intervals pulled over on the roadside grass, or dirt, or sand, waiting for gaps in traffic. But I'm patient: this is just part of the journey, part of travelling by Bikecar, part of the process.

I pulled into the delightful town of Apalachicola and was almost instantly offered a free meal by two men sat outside of the Hole In The Wall Seafood restaurant. One of them, the owner, said that each day they selected someone to sit at the Captain's Table, which I soon found out meant that I could sit at whatever table I wanted and would be served the meal and drink of my choice. It was a delightful little place full of character, and the Gumbo with a plate of oysters was pretty good too. Set up by the husband and wife team of Jeff and Debi Fletcher, each knot in the wood planked walls had a painting of some kind of eye behind it, and Jeff pointed at a heart tattoo on the bar that read Jeff + Debi, saying 'I put seven of these around the place when we refurbished it, Debi has only found four so far, it really pisses her off, in a good way.'

I thanked my new friends and pushed on a few more miles, then a few more, wondering exactly where I'd camp that night. The road after Apalachicola was mostly causeway or bridge connecting small islands, which were quiet but just a little too built up for me to surreptitiously pitch my shelter. Just when I feared I'd be pedalling into darkness – something I really didn't want to do – a camping site appeared to my left. I rode in and cast a watchful eye over the trailers, all of them in a state of disrepair.

There didn't appear to be a camp office and the toilet block had a large hole in the roof and a sign outside that read *Don't Even Think About It*. Eventually I found some humans; two fairly similar, pot bellied men sat by a campfire, swatting away mosquitos with one hand and cradling a can of beer in the other. 'Ummm, hey!' I said, as they both stared at me in disbelief, as if a red headed bloke on a Bikecar didn't stop by every day. 'Do you guys know if I can camp here? I'll be up super early, just wanted to get off the road.'

'Sure you can,' said one of the men, pointing at the football field-sized area of empty grass, 'what the hell is that you're on?'

'It's a Bikecar, her name is Priscilla,' I said proudly.

'Where you from?'

'England. But this journey started in Memphis.'

'You pedalled from Memphis on that?'

'More or less,' I said, grinning. 'Hey, is there a camp manager around I need to speak to?'

'He's not here, but I'll try and call him.'

'Thanks.' I pedalled off and set up my tent, then

returned to the fire. 'My name's Dave,' I said, stretching out a hand.

'Bobby,' said the first man with a shake.

'Bobby,' said the second man, too.

'Are you brothers?' I asked, trying not to laugh.

'Yup, oh and here's our sister's boy,' one of them said as this young kid with a shaved head and dirt all over his face strolled over like the cock of the walk, his wide eyes focused on the Bikecar.

'Your name's not Bobby, is it?' I asked the kid. He turned his head and looked at me like I'd just run over his pet raccoon,

'How did ya know that?' he asked, shocked.

'Guys, really?' I looked at the kid and then the two men, 'are you having me on? You all have the same name?'

'Yup, Mom said it made things easier,' Bobby Number Two told me, 'but young Bobby here, man he can take his beer.'

'His beer?'

'He'll put a six pack down like you've never seen,'

'But…' I paused, bewildered, 'how old is he?'

'I'm eight,' said Little Bobby, challenging me. I had nothing left to offer, and instead gave Little Bobby a ride in my Bikecar for being a bigger man than me, although he did have to sit right on the edge of the passenger seat to reach the pedals.

A phone rang. 'Camp Manager on the line!' shouted one of the big Bobby's.

'I'm not even going to ask *his* name,' I said, walking over, 'can you ask him how much it is to camp for a night.'

There was a conversation.

'Twenty five bucks,' Bobby reported.

'Excuse me?' I spluttered, 'are you serious? For a tent?'

Another conversation on the phone.

'He'll go down to twenty two…'

'Is there breakfast included?' I joked,

Bobby ignored that, but said, 'The shower's broken, but there's plumbing on one of the shitters now, and there's running water from the faucet.'

I looked around: at my Bikecar, my erected Sky Tent, the falling apart trailers in the park, each one of the three Bobbys. There was nothing there that convinced me to part with twenty-two dollars. 'Sorry guys, I'm going to move on, that's a bit steep for me,' I said, hoping they'd take pity on me and start being reasonable.

'Good luck,' they all said in unison, raising a beer. That included the little one.

I left the park shaking my head but feeling strangely glad that I'd just had that Deliverance-like experience. I resolved never to call one of my future children Bobby, pedalled past a sign warning of bears, and a few minutes later and under the cover of darkness, found a patch of grass in a copse for which I'd be charged absolutely nothing for a night's sleep.

21

Perry, Florida

A storm blew all night and sleep was intermittent, partly down to the howling wind and rain and partly due to the fact that I wasn't lying on my sleeping mat and didn't realise. I'd made camp in a littered, buggy space just off the road and several mosquitos had found their way into my Sky Tent, as they do when one sets up after dark. I scratched mercilessly throughout dawn, waiting for enough light to make my move.

The clouds were broody and threatened more than rain but it didn't arrive. Instead, four eagles circled high overhead, tracing my progress for more than an hour. Come to think of it, they might have been vultures.

The quiet little village of Carabelle was guarded by a surreptitious restaurant with *2Al's* scribbled on a sign above the door, a hidden gem with the best breakfast I'd had in months. There was little change in the landscape once the highway branched away from the Gulf, forging inland in a horseshoe around the swamps of Saint George Sound and Apalachee Bay. I rode near-clear roads through

Ochlockonee River State Park and then took a break at the wonderfully named Sopchoppy, where buck toothed locals looked hungrily at the perfect dental work exhibited by out-of-towners who honoured the gas station with five minutes of coffee time before trailing their shiny boats to lucky, distant waters.

Highway 98 was now a shadow of its ruthless former self, a lonely one-lane-each-way dribble through the northern Florida badlands. Hundreds of two-inch caterpillars commuted across the road, necessitating the occasional life-preserving swerve and keeping me focused when otherwise I would have dosed off, one eye on the wing mirror, one on the miles clicking by on the GPS. I took a break at a muddy picnic spot, grateful that the rumbling of Priscilla's wheels forced a small gator to vacate the riverside clearing, and reclining on a wooden picnic bench I followed commentary of the final half an hour of the English Premier League season.

Not to be confused with American Football, which bizarrely is a game mostly involving hands and not feet, football used to be my favourite thing in the world. I still love the game, but since I left my previous life football is now more of an appreciation than a passion. Still, I was more than amped up for Manchester United - who I've followed since they were relegation candidates in the 80s -

to record a result better than their City neighbours in order to claim a record 20th title. Remarkably, as is so often the case in football, what seemed likely proved to not be the case, and to my (and that of several other million people around the world) great disappointment City scored twice in the final minutes of the season to claim the championship. Once upon a time, with my field of interests narrower, this kind of thing would have been devastating, leaving me low for days. As it was, I shrugged, popped some jelly babies into my mouth then rode back out on the asphalt to concentrate on not squishing caterpillars. There are more important things in life than football, and I was making tracks towards the most valuable thing of all.

*   *   *

Em had finished her Business Excellence course and been rewarded for her efforts with a delightful little Minnie Mouse cap with ears. An old school friend of hers just happened to be driving from nearby Orlando back to Tallahassee, Florida. Em had hitched a ride and as she drove north west I was now riding due east, for once both of us itching for a collision.

They met me on the outskirts of Perry, Florida, and Em introduced me to her friend Rhi, and her Dad, Gareth. Rhi, a former professional gymnast, was already dressed for exercise and jumped onto the Bikecar eagerly. We rode the 8 miles through town and by the time we reached the KOA campsite in the southern suburbs Gareth and Em had a BBQ going, a box of Mexican beer and a huge pile of steaks just waiting to be devoured. I was in heaven.

And then the sky cracked, thunder boomed and rain began to fall. We all moved under a small picnic shelter across from our hut and chewed hungrily. There's a chance that in addition to my own steak I had half of Em's and bit of Gareth's, too. In a very manly way Gareth had a fascination with my calves which, still unnaturally large thanks to four and a half thousand miles on a skateboard, were now hardened and angular from Bikecar pedalling. 'I've never seen anything like them!' proclaimed Gareth. It took me back to my post skating days, when the right calf was ballooned Hulk-like out of proportion to the left and people in London would roll up their trouser legs to compare their own, inordinately skinny and pale chicken legs. Isn't it bizarre, how humans find satisfaction or amazement in physical differences when each and every one of us is unique?

Calves aside, it was filling my stomach that was of major concern; I swear taste buds are more sensitive after a day of good, hard exercise. Eventually the food and beer ran out and Rhi and Gareth scrambled into the car to make a getaway in the rain. With a wave goodbye, they were gone. Em and I cleared up and retreated inside our 12 foot by 12 foot Kabin. Yes, in KOA campsites cabins have a K, and they also like to cover their beds in a sheet of plastic. This wouldn't do, so we trotted to the office and shamelessly used our English accents to extract some proper sheets and pillows from the staff. It's amazing how much traction an English accent gets in America, so naturally if you're blessed with the dulcet tones of the Mother Tongue you play on every, glorious English syllable when in pursuit of something. Brilliantly, there seems to be an assumption that not only will you almost certainly know someone's friend 'who once spent a week in London', but you're also very much a part of the Royal Family. It took me several months of wasting time explaining that England is actually quite big and that very few people have ever seen the Queen up close, before the realisation that I could answer 'yes, I know your friend John, we go way back,' and 'I'm good friends with Wills and Harry, and Queenie is a hoot!' without so much as a second question.

Em and I left the campsite only once those two days, to fetch more coals and supplies for another BBQ from a gas station across the road. We were kept off the mini golf course by poor weather, opted out of table tennis because it was impossible to hug each other while playing, and took a couple of visits to the swimming pool. A short lady with one, bizarrely central front tooth, had been tasked with cleaning our Kabin and it took some explanation that 'no, we were quite at ease in our own mess.' Her smiley face seemed initially upset, and although it was difficult to understand what she was saying to us with a deliciously squeaky voice we slowly felt a rapport growing, and our relationship continued without many words, just winks and smiles.

On paper, two days in a KOA campsite might not be classed as romantic, especially when you consider that at all times the air in Perry smelled distinctly of cabbage, a legacy of the chemical process used by the local pulp mill which the locals positively translated as 'smelling like money'. But despite this whole crazy world around us nothing else mattered. We were cocooned within our cabin within arms reach of everything that we needed.

We giggled endlessly, exchanged stories from the road with tales from Disney World, and became sponges for each other's company, touch and conversation. It always happened when we were together, other people drifted into shadows and seeing the sights became irrelevant. Even when we both settled down at our laptops to catch up on work, blog writing and video editing, there was wonderful comfort at being in such close proximity to my best friend. And that's what we were, well on our way to becoming soul mates just six months on from being total strangers.

22

Manatees & the Trail

I spent an extra day in Perry after Em left, heavy storms throwing up a thick spray on the highway, which I could see clearly from the front of the Kabin. A torrent of log trucks kept the road busy and the reduced visibility meant an increased lack of safety. I wanted to be ready for the challenge ahead so happily settled down for another day of rest, the only sadness being a heart-shaped hole left behind by Em's departure. Perry was about 535 miles from my starting point at Crystal Springs, Mississipi, and I figured I was now a little bit past the halfway mark and had less than a fortnight's pedal to Miami, should everything proceed uninterrupted. Having Em waiting at the finish lane gave me extra purpose and incentive to focus on Miami but her support, also combined with regular contact through text and daily calls, gave me wings. I was free to enjoy the journey and make the most of my moments on the road, as well as having someone to deeply share those memories with, even from afar.

In fact, my next target would be a town called Crystal

River, Florida, where Em had a friend who ran a business taking people to swim with manatees. With just two days to cover 115 miles I was going to have to fast scrub away my rest day rust and hope conditions were to my favour. Luckily, they were. There wasn't much traffic as I headed south from Perry, and the road was wide and comfortable with little wind. The sun shone brightly and eagles swooped overhead, small snakes wriggled back into the grass from their bathing spots on the side of the asphalt and armadillos snuffled around in the grassy verge looking for breakfast, completely oblivious to my presence.

I fielded confused questions at a remote gas station from a bloke in a Hummer who couldn't understand why I'd chosen to pedal a long way, politely ignored a cowboy who told me that the road I was on was legendary for the nails which pierced bicycle tyres, and took strange delight in a truck with a bed full of felled palm trees. This truly was a tropical paradise. At Cross City I took a break in a McDonalds, watching a group of kids move cautiously around the Bikecar out in the parking lot. I rarely had qualms about leaving Priscilla unattended. I could lock the storage box and always took the GPS and camera with me, and she was such a weird contraption nobody ever went close enough to steal anything, they were always stuck in amazement or confusion – brilliant emotions for reducing a human's thieving capacity.

Across the road from McDonalds I was delighted to find the beginning of another off-road cycle track, the Nature Coast Trail giving me almost 30 miles of peace during which I saw only three other bicycles and just a couple of pedestrians. What bliss! One of the final acts of the day was to cross over the Suwannee River at Fanning, a glorious truss bridge providing the perfect viewing platform from which I could see enormous Sturgeon jumping from the river, creating dynamite-like explosions that rose ten feet into the air. Silent and menacing, two large alligators rested still on a mud bank down below, no doubt wishing they could jump so athletically. I made a mental note not to camp close to water and instead found my night's base beside a trail picnic bench in a dark section of wood.

Despite hours of rain the sky was clear by the time I set off the next morning, enjoying the final 7 miles of cycle path before rejoining the main highway at Chiefland and powering across flat woodland and farms, reaching Crystal River before dusk and treating myself to a $60 motel room - and the shower that came with it. I was now at my most southerly point all journey and the temperatures were growing noticeably, the air becoming muggier. I pedalled with a leather cushion behind me, a choice of lumber and back support that allowed no ventilation whatsoever. It took just a few minutes of effort for the back of my shirt to become sodden and the humid air was now preventing my clothes from drying fast. At the start of this venture I'd been relatively unfit and my body odour reflected my body's surprise at such a sudden – then continual – cleansing of its pores, regular exercise changing and subsequently decreasing my natural scent as the days went on.

After 650 miles my sweat was healthy and almost unnoticeable, but the wet shirts hung over the back of the passenger seat and tied to my flagpoles did start to pong a bit when they remained damp for too long. I took all my clothes into the shower with me that night in Crystal River, gave them a good scrub, and set the fan on high before heading out to explore the town and find myself a fish dinner.

For all the challenges of riding on the road this journey had been splashed with little moments of magic. From chance encounters with wildlife, witnessing beautiful scenery, discovering strange American customs or indeed finding people to join me for a stretch on the Bikecar; the dangers and fatigue and battles with traffic were all made worth it by unforeseen gems. None of these were more

248

satisfying than those wallowing in Crystal River, Florida. Em's friend Bill had a nickname, Bird, and so it was that I found myself lingering at some godawful hour outside Bird's Underwater Dive Centre with a few other travellers, all eager for the encounter to come that morning.

We were kitted up with wetsuit, mask, fins and snorkel in the Dive Shop, surrounded by t-shirts that had slogans like 'Crystal River, quaint little drinking village with a manatee problem', then we were ushered onto a launch boat which took us out into Kings Bay. We stopped as soon as our guide Rhonda spotted the first manatee and everyone slipped into the water, gasping at the slight chill. Visibility was low at that point and I could barely make out the faint outline of an adult manatee and a repetitive *chomp chomp chomp* as it hoovered along the bed. Rhonda didn't wait long before deciding to take us to a new spot, a decision that earned her quite a few tips that day. In fact, it was one of the guests on board who spotted the female manatee and her calf as they quietly grazed along the edges of the channel, either side of which were residences and private boats.

We spent the next hour in amazement, observing these incredible mammals at close quarters. Bird's is not the only company who offers such an experience but they are forerunners in preserving the safety and habitat of the manatees, who are drawn to the warm spring waters of Crystal River for much of the year. We'd been told never to aggressively approach a manatee, only to be still and calm, never swim over the top of one, and only touch if the manatee is comfortable enough to come close. The mother, her length around nine feet, and her calf slowly took a shine to our group, eventually getting so friendly I was able to reach out and gently tickle under the little one's flipper pits, causing him to barrel roll blissfully several times. It was a gorgeous moment, so peaceful beneath the surface, a momentary connection with these gentle giants who sometimes stealthily appeared alongside and beneath us without warning, then hugged each other reassuringly before returning for more tickles.

They seemed so comfortable in human company but it is this very nature that threatens the manatee. Most companies in the region promote ethical behaviour but lessening the impact of human interaction can be tricky with hundreds of swimmers - often inexperienced - lowering themselves into the water from tour boats each day. The boats themselves are required to navigate slowly and carefully down marked channels but of the ten or so manatees that I saw that day not one of them, including three calves, boasted untainted skin. Scars were rife across the backs, flippers and paddle-like tail; so strange seeing such a gentle creature covered in battle scars, all a product of careless humans. Dolphins briefly joined us in the channel before we were pointed up a tiny through-stream that opened up into the pristine Three Sister Springs. Colourful fish darted around as large Blue Crab scuttled along the bed of the pool. I followed instructions that Em had issued me by slowly breaching the surface to see a half and half view through my mask: below the surface was infinitely clear water, above was a thriving circle of trees, plants and flowers. A little paradise hidden away; right in the middle of a small town.

On the way back down the adjoining channel two adult manatees, each at least ten feet long, pushed their way past in the opposite direction, brushing all of the way down the side of my body, the natural wake left by their bulk throwing me around temporarily. Such a special, glorious moment, they didn't even know I was there, so focused they were on chewing the now sparse sea grass below. An incoming hoard of three boatloads of snorkelers and a small armada of kayakers signalled the end of our session, there's a reason why Bird's ask their clients to arrive early. I rose out of the water for the final time, grateful for the waiting bottle of water and snacks, knowing that this was a morning that would stay long in my memory.

*   *   *

'Let me tell ya, live your life while you're young, do what you do, enjoy yourself.'

The woman from behind the gas station counter rested a plastic cup on a fine, round belly between slurps on her coffee, as she lectured me on how to live life to the fullest. I chuckled, 'I'll be living my life when I'm old, too!'

'Good for you!' She proclaimed, before adding, 'There's nothing like freedom, get on the road and go, good for you.'

'Have you ever done something like this?' I asked, curiously,

She took a final sip of coffee, 'Nope, thought about it when I was younger but….' she paused, lamenting, '…you know, things get in the way.'

I'd waited a bit too long in Crystal River, reveling in the post-manatee ambience, showing Bird and his team Priscilla and watching them ride around the car park. 'It's tough to pedal!' said one of them, 'what a great idea.' By the time I hit the road it was approaching 5pm and rush hour was thriving. This, plus ten miles of roadworks, meant that my progress was limited for much of the day's remaining light. Eventually, completely unexpected and unannounced by my map, a perfectly smooth and wide cycle path appeared at the side of the highway and I turned onto it with a whoop of joy. My face, hands and bare arms were covered in the grime that typically surrounds thick traffic but I revelled in the freedom of having my own path, even if my off-coast route towards the centre of the State meant that my idea of Florida as a flat place was now an ancient ideal.

Through the pleasant Citrus Hills, where a guffawing troop of psychiatric nurses offered me a free bed for the night in the local hospital, and on to the rather putrid town of Hernando, which was one of those places that you wish you'd never seen. It was almost dark and I considered renting a cheap motel room but shadowy characters lingered on every corner and sinister noises emerged from the rooms by which I pedalled. I continued out of town and picked up supplies in a rundown gas station, the miserable git of an owner telling me that although the Withlacoochee cycle trail stretched south for the next 40 miles, the chances of me surviving the night were slim. 'Gypsies everywhere in these woods,' he said, shaking his head. 'Camp far off the path into the woods, don't let them see you, won't think twice about slitting your throat.' I decided that I didn't need to tell him that it wasn't easy foraging too far off the beaten path on a Bikecar and thanked him for his advice, to which he replied, 'you heard of the Brown Recluse spider? They're everywhere in these woods, don't let one bite you, you'll be dead by morning.'

I made a mental note to return to Hernando once I'd exhausted every bit of joy that life had to give and needed somewhere to claim my last breaths. It was almost as if bad karma spread from the old man around his entire property, because it took me twenty minutes and plenty of sweaty heaving to finally persuade Priscilla up and over a muddy hillock behind the gas station, the Bikecar's long wheelbase threatening to ground the chain into the narrow ridge. I was thoroughly pissed off at proceedings by the time I made it down to the cycle path and pedalled a good three miles before being satisfied that I could camp beside the path in relative peace without being murdered. I figured the old man had probably never travelled this far from his hometown, and as he was the only person likely to cause me harm I should be fine.

As it was, the only disturbance of the night came just as I'd shuffled down into my sleeping bag, only to be greeted by an almighty siren and the familiar red, blue and white flashing lights of a patrol car. 'Hands up!' came the shout, so I obeyed, naturally. *This isn't even remotely funny*, I thought as the official approached, purposefully blinding me with his flashlight. 'What are you doing here?' he asked, firmly. I explained my situation and my mission and eventually he told me to bring my arms down. 'There's a big fine for anyone camping on the trace,' he said thoughtfully, making me wish he'd shot me in the first place.

'Honestly officer, I had no idea camping was forbidden, I've just reached the area and felt unsafe continuing through the darkness,' I said, pleadingly, still expecting him to issue me with a piece of paper that I could use to start my next campfire. Thankfully, he backed down.

'In future, ask permission if you think you might need to camp on a path like this.'

'I will, absolutely, thank you for understanding.'

'Yup, we're not all bad down here,' he said, smiling for the first time in our brief conversation, 'good luck and stay safe.'

And with that he was off, his prowling, intimidating lights bouncing off the trees as his patrol continued.

*   *   *

I'd begun to take down camp the next morning when I saw my first human of the day. The old man on a recumbent bicycle didn't respond to my raised palm, well, not immediately anyway. I watched him as he passed, hunkered down, pretending not to see me. Then, thirty metres later he slowed, his shoulders released from their hunch and he circled back. 'I'm sorry,' he said, 'I thought it a bit strange that someone was camped here, I thought you were a gypsy.'

'I suppose I am, in a way!' I smiled and reached out a hand, 'I'm Dave.'

'Dick,' he said, returning the shake with a fingerless glove, 'I realised that a gypsy probably wouldn't have a…a, what do you call that exactly?' He nodded his head in Priscilla's direction.

'It's a Bikecar, I'm heading to Miami.'

'Well, I'd like to treat you to breakfast, there's a whole crowd of people in Floral City, ten miles down the trail.'

'I never turn down breakfast, Dick,' I replied, and quickly sped up my packing.

I'd happened upon a brand new world. The life that designated cycle trails bring to a region is just breathtaking. Just as nature alongside the path was protected and introduced to the public by small, informative signs, the path itself was a hive of activity, a lifeline to recreation and fitness. There were more cyclists in that hour-long pedal to Floral City than I had seen in the entirety of my journey so far: countless three wheeled trikes were in action, as well as recumbent bikes, normal bicycles and other folks on roller blades and longboards. In Floral City we rode a few metres off the trail and parked up next to the Shamrocks café. Inside waited a group of over 20 middle-aged pedallers, all wearing tight shorts and luminous yellow t-shirts, and they were most amused when Dick walked in with someone he'd 'picked up from the Trail.' This was a weekly Saturday morning event, all of these friends amassing first for a catch-up over eggs and toast and then a group ride on the Withlacoochee. I was made most welcome, especially by an older lady who offered to sit on my lap for the rest of the journey.

The local riding craze seemed to revolve around one shop, Hampton's Edge cycles in Floral City. The owner Regis showed me around, not quite realising how dangerous it was introducing me to so many brilliantly functional modes of non motorised transport. Even during the short while I was there the shop had a stream of customers, all smiling and looking forward to a day's riding in the sun. It was the perfect example of how a community is enriched by the pleasures of recreational provision; just a simple cycle trail and a friendly place to buy and fix gear, and the whole town was thriving.

It was a glorious day riding along the trail, exchanging

waves and curious glances with pedallers, soaking up the sun and rewarding myself with an ice cream each time the trail ran through a village. Deer, eagles and squirrels were frequent sights, but I was delighted to discover Gopher Tortoises every mile or so, sometimes pottering around in the verge, sometimes sleeping right in the middle of the path. I've always felt an affinity to tortoises, possibly due to the shared wrinkles around our eyes, maybe because they too travelled slow and with apparent purpose. I parked up on a quiet section of track and lay down next to one of them for a while, feeling a sense of connected satisfaction as he cautiously poked his head out from within his shell, took me in and accepted my company. Both of us lay still and prone, arms folded in beneath our chests side by side.

Eventually the trail ended and I made my way back into dangerous territory, the highway to Dade City strewn with weekend traffic. I opted to trundle south along slower, parallel roads around the back of the city and was rewarded with a rollercoaster ride, consistent with ups and downs. Long, fifteen minute, one mile per hour climbs were evened out with one minute long, 20 mile per hour descents. Again, and again, reeling in the miles, unstoppably fit now, legs fully accustomed to pedalling from an upright, seated position against 8% gradients on rough, potholed roads. Once again I was ready to jump fences, a naturally earned and completely free side effect of taking on this adventure. This is my drug, my addiction. Eventually, after a brief fried chicken stop in a Shell Garage the other side of Dade, where the man who served me rushed outside to thrust a free bottle of Coke into my hands, Priscilla and I celebrated passing the journey's 700 mile mark with a violent orange sunset, opting to camp beneath an overhanging tree in the grounds of a Baptist Church.

23

Across the Middle

I'd chosen my path simply, taking a line equidistant from the true cities of Orlando to the east and Tampa to the west, figuring that the furthest I could get from enormous urban areas the less likely it was that I'd end up as road kill. Of course, the logic is skewed a little as it takes just one out of control driver to ruin your day in either city or mid country, but although the density of my speeding metallic friends increased around small towns my route over the spine of Florida was far more comfortable than it had been along the built-up Gulf Coast.

With the increased strength of my body came a capacity for greater distances and on the 21st day of the journey, exactly three weeks after I'd restarted the venture at the Exxon Garage in Crystal Springs, Mississippi, I recorded the longest daily haul of the expedition. Clocking up just under 60 miles on the Bikecar roughly translated to a 200 mile day on an average touring bicycle. I was hulking 450lbs including my own body weight, my speed was limited by a low gearing system and I averaged about 8 miles an hour on a really good day of clear roads. With each daily dot placed on my journey map I was inching closer to Miami and my intentions were clear with the red line slowly arrowing across Florida towards the east coast. As with most journeys the last leg was always going to be toughest and most fraught with danger. I wanted to avoid the heavily built-up coast north of Miami and planned to stay as central as possible until the very last moment, when I'd enter the city from the west. My options were low because of the limited routes through the Everglades National Park in Southern Florida but I'd have to deal with that when the time came. For now, I was content with a diagonal route splicing the centre of the State, far away from the glowing edges depicted by a nighttime satellite image of Florida.

It was the countryside that I enjoyed most, but those brief, sweaty sojourns into urbania were worth the effort. They say that as you go further south in Florida the mentality becomes more northern, which is another way to suggest that the upper reaches of Florida are populated by a bunch of chainsaw-loving shit kickers. Apart from the odd exception the stereotype was accurate as I decreased my latitude down the wide-open centre. This was the habitat of grumpy, bitter conspiracy theorists who felt no responsibility for their own situation and put blame at the feet of the government. Racial insinuations were regularly made towards the chap in charge; Rosa Parks' legacy hadn't reached this far south, yet. Fast food restaurants rarely had empty slots in the parking lot outside. A bandana-clad gas station attendant whispered during a brief conversation, 'You're not in Florida right now, you're in Polk County. Sister county to all inbred places in America.'

One short, mostly blissful ride down a seemingly innocuous 4-mile cycle path was interrupted by several rounds of gunfire, which ripped through the trees around me. I jumped off Priscilla and crouched behind the storage box, mystified and thoroughly pissed off. It would be bloody typical if this journey through the American South was cut short by a wandering bullet. I definitely expected no correlation between someone whose hobby involved guns and their awareness of a recreational trail nearby, so couldn't be sure if there was a hunt going on, or if there was a signpost nearby that seemed to make a sufficient target.

Eventually I caught sight of the shooter, a woman with a large rifle who was apparently firing at some inanimate object at the bottom of her garden, and I thoroughly attribute my subsequent progress - at the highest flatland speeds of the journey - to her. Having been close enough to see hanging twigs shattered and bark blown out of tree trunks just a short distance from my position, the sad ease of lost life was crystalised and I wasn't fond of becoming just another statistic, purposeful or not. I don't wish to adopt this as a typically dramatic 'I got shot at' moment, rather, I'm happy to admit that I metaphorically shat myself and escaped as fast as possible. And then it began to rain.

In between dodging bullets and random gas station conversations were long periods in *the zone*, a part meditative state when nothing but thoughts accompanied the now natural state of pedalling. At times when I hadn't fed or watered myself enough my concentration waned towards doubt, a battle between pessimism and common sense. Priscilla was a juggernaut equipped with great inertia when up to speed. A physics teacher might suggest that it would take months for a high-flying Bikecar to stop, such is its bulk, but during my lowest ebbs of energy I'd convince myself that all was not good. Why am I going slower than usual? There must be something wrong? I'd pick out a weird squeaking or imagine a frustrating wobble in the wheel right in front of me, convinced that these were the foibles responsible for my fast deceleration.

My moods were so flowing, a tide of delight rushing

towards frustration, then pulled back out by a moon of optimism. As always, the friction was coming from my brain, not the Bikecar, and my habitual affirmative attitude was a crucial lubricant essential to setting me back on track. After all, if I was going slow at least I was still moving. My travels had taught me this, through all the grind and pain and mental disgust at an approaching hill on a day of extreme temperatures, the knowledge that there was always a better feeling waiting to be earned kept me going. When stuff gets rough, fatigue forcing temples to squeeze in and corners of mouth to drag down, simple things like sleep, friendship and an appreciation of basics offer refocus and resilience.

Whether on or outside of an expedition, adventure had given me the tools to defeat the negativity that once sucked my life dry. If things were always rosy we wouldn't be able to appreciate the tint in the spectacles and although on occasion we might be overcome by hopelessness, remembering that there will inevitably be brighter moments provides a solution.

Warthogs dashing through roadside copses, cavalcades of motorcycles, sweet smelling flowers around the blue, rippled pools in the centre of Lakeland and Priscilla's diminutive stature when parked up against huge American trucks: all memories that overcame the less fun dashes across major junctions and pavement-crawls alongside highways too busy to join properly. I crashed for a night in Fort Meade, glowing from a long day on the road and my last experience of the day; two cop cars pulling up either side of Priscilla for a photograph.

Most days I pulled over to the roadside at a pre-arranged time to speak to a reporter or radio station that had an interest in my adventures. Shortly after I passed the 800-mile mark National Geographic radio gave me a call and as I chatted away about life on a Bikecar a rusty old car pulled up nearby. A small group of grubby youngsters unloaded themselves from the vehicle and began slinking around, assuming an intimidating manner.

'Nothing is ever expected on these journeys,' I said into the phone, 'in fact, as we talk I'm slowly being surrounded by a group of drug addicts. I apologise in advance if I have to go and deal with some trouble!'

'Can you describe your current situation?' asked Boyd, the presenter.

'Well,' I whispered, 'I'm close to a fairly ramshackle gas station and these reprobates have just emerged from a car that doesn't seem roadworthy. I daresay they're eyeing up my Bikecar less with curiosity than an eagerness to discover spare parts for their own vehicle.'

'Does this kind of thing happen to you often?'

'Honestly, not really. The Bikecar draws interest from most, but this is the first time this journey that I've been surrounded by a bunch of hooligans.'

Eventually the interview drew to a close and I thanked Justin, the chuckling producer, before turning to face the group, who were hovering uncomfortably near Priscilla. 'What do you think of my vehicle?' I asked them jovially.

'Does it have a motor?' growled a skinny young man with several scars on his arm.

'Nope, just my legs,' I replied.

'You got to be in good shape!' said one of the girls, drawing laughter from the other females. The men stared at me with hatred.

'What's it like living in Sebring?' I directed my question at the original man.

'Boring!' screeched one of the girls. More laughter. 'You got some good abs, there,' she continued.

'I can't really see how you could possibly know that,' I said, tugging on my t-shirt.

'How far you come?'

'Memphis.'

'You never did!'

'True story.'

'You got some nice calves though, they hairy…'

'They're not hairy because I've cycled a long way,

they're hairy because I'm a male. Anyway, I gotta get going to Miami.'

'You peddlin' that to Miami?!'

'All the way!'

'Be safe! Plus I love your accent, you from Australia?'

'Please tell me you are joking,' I spoke with my finest English accent as I lowered myself onto Priscilla and pedalled off with haste, offering a friendly wave to Sebring's finest.

As with the progression of every journey, a couple hundred more distant friends joined the ranks on Facebook, and it was one such person that gave me focus for the next stage across Florida. At some point in 2011 I had received a spate of friend requests from various Cornthwaite's around the world, most of them on their own quest to add new branches to the family tree. Of course, not one of them turned out to be direct family but this didn't seem to hinder Mary Cornthwaite Winger, who messaged me saying she'd been following the Bikecar journey, was really happy that I hadn't been killed by that car outside Memphis, and that I was welcome to spend a night at her place south of Sebring. Mary and her husband Tommy met me at the top of their driveway and Mary hopped onto Priscilla to help guide me back to the property, a bungalow tucked up beside a neat garden. Around the back was a huge shed surrounded by motorcycles and a plethora of cars, some shiny and new looking, others no more than shells. It's fair to say Tommy was a dab hand at mechanical stuff, and I secretly hoped he'd give Priscilla a once over before I left.

'Here's your home away from home,' said Mary, showing me to a trailer behind the house, right next to a lovely deck and a perfectly round above ground swimming pool. Inside the trailer a little pile of gifts awaited, a box of Cornflakes - my cereal namesake, some bananas, milk, orange juice and a joyous, familiar tub of chocolaty goodness.

For years I've been on a tongue-in-cheek mission to be sponsored by Nutella. I love the stuff and would be quite happy to survive forever on a diet of hazelnut-flavoured chocolate spread. Even the thought of it makes my heart sing, and it's rare that I'll create a video these days without a small bit of product placement, even though I've not been lucky enough to have even one reply to countless messages and partnership proposals. Yes, Nutella continue to rebuff my advances for a professional relationship bolstered by a lifetime supply but despite this, I am so open about my love of the brown stuff that a strange kind of pseudo sponsorship has occurred. Even strangers, those ghost-like social media friends with whom I had made no direct contact until a journey takes me into their neighbourhood, often welcome me into their homes with a hearty 'Go take a shower, and here's some Nutella.' This is why I travel, not for the Nutella, but because endless kindness is evident when you pull back the duvet of complacency and peek underneath. The glee on people's face when they see my own light up, Mary and Tommy stood beaming in the doorway as I cradled their present gratefully, before I attacked each of my hosts with a hearty hug.

It may now come as a surprise to you, but my love for Nutella was surpassed by Mary's love for animals. Walking into their house was a canine gauntlet and for me, with my innate distress at small dogs, being surrounded by several yapping Chihuahuas as they slipped and scrapped on a shiny, polished floor was as close to hell as was possible. Just inside the front door an enormous cat laid flat out on its back, bothered not by the noise pollution created by its diminutive housemates. 'I've no idea where they all came from!' Mary offered, her hands in the air, 'but Pinky has a Facebook page.'

'Where do you find all of these animals, Mary?' I asked,

'Well, they find me,' she said, her face full of love,

'Sure they do,' I mocked, winking at her to let her know

I was only half joking, 'so you're just walking along and they come up to you and you accidentally put them into your car, right…?'

There was no doubt that Mary was the protagonist of this mid-Florida kennel but Tommy clearly had his own fondness for the pups, although he disguised it well. Mary had just finished telling me which dogs she'd most bonded with and that none of them liked Tommy's work boots when Tommy pointed at a small brown thing at my feet, 'That's Benny, he's the little'est.' I looked at Benny and it looked back, a tiny little tongue seemingly stuck out of its mouth. I was tempted to give it a pull but refrained. By then Mary had picked up a white dog,

'I used to take her over to my Dad's with me every week, until Dad got the electric wheelchair…' a pause '…and then I feared for her life.'

A few minutes had passed and by now some of the animals had grown confident enough to start licking my ankles, which was perturbing. The only thing worse than a small dog is a fearless small dog, I felt the pack slowly circling, getting closer, surrounding us. Surrounding me!

'People keep calling and the next thing you know there's one, there's eight, I don't know,' Mary shrugged, but she wasn't doing a great job of convincing me that her animal collection was accidental. 'We had kids once,' Mary told me, 'but we had to get rid of them because of the dogs.'

'That seems fair,' I replied.

'This one is definitely very special,' she said, pointing at one.

'When you say, special?' I asked, cunningly.

'Yeah, special,' Mary said, 'he's very sweet and he has epilepsy, so…'

'Oh, literally?' I choked, foot in my mouth.

We may not have exactly shared every passion but Mary and Tommy were the perfect hosts. Funny, grounded and generous, they understood my need for rest and carried on with their daily lives while I slept and edited. I walked out of my trailer to find Priscilla not in the spot that I'd left her. On closer inspection she was discovered up off the ground on Tommy's electric car lift, having had a little make-over. Tommy was in his element and had tightened bits here, added some grease there. 'If this wasn't man-powered we could make a lot of modifications,' he grinned, responding to my query about her condition with a simple, 'she'll make it.'

Up on the wall was a sign that read *Winger's ESSO*, and as Tommy continued pottering about his garage my discomfort at being surrounded by oilcans and engine parts and heavy tools grew. I found myself standing taller, straightening my back and puffing my chest out, basically trying in vain to appear more manly. I shared this with Tommy, who answered, 'Nah, there's not a lot to it,' which didn't make me feel better. Mary did a more convincing job.

'I've been around mechanics all my life…' she pondered, '…and my brain wanders off, thinking, do the Chihuahuas need to be fed?' She rounded off the cameo by adding a sticker to the growing collection on Priscilla's storage box, which read *Real men love Chihuahuas.*

From a walk around Mary's garden, which was home to several geckos and small memorials to past pets, to a mealtime ride into Sebring in Tommy's modified 1954 Ford Customline, I couldn't have felt more at home with the Cornthwaite-Wingers. We may not have been genetic relatives but it felt like saying goodbye to family when I prepared to pull out. One of the cats even climbed onto the Bikecar's passenger seat as I pedalled the first few metres down the driveway to the front gate, where Tommy gave me a firm handshake and Mary smothered me in a hug, her body shaking with emotion. 'Now I know how your Mum feels when you go off on these adventures,' she whispered, tears in her eyes, 'please be safe.' I was choking up and didn't look back after our last wave goodbye.

With a tough pedal up the sandy, steep driveway I wondered what thoughts were going through their minds as they watched me leave, yet again I was a brief apparition, in and out of someone's life after an intense acquaintance and a too-soon farewell. My sadness slowly fell once I'd reconvened with sealed road and the miles took me away from new friends, and I longed already for a return road trip, hopefully with Em, so I could introduce her to the people who had made such an impact on my journey.

24

Gates and Glades

I moved swiftly in a southwesterly direction, progress fast until I found myself a heartbreakingly distance down a bike path before encountering a yellow gate blocking the way. It was locked and it seemed there was no way past. I couldn't bear the idea of retracing tracks and adding 15 miles to my route on busy roads, so I made use of the Internet on my phone and called around, eventually persuading someone from the Florida Department of Environmental Protection to provide an 'open sesame'. When he eventually arrived the Ranger didn't have much information about the trail ahead but seemed sure that there were no more gates, which put me at ease.

I'd waited an hour and a half for access beyond the gate and now hoped for a nice, smooth path all the way to my night's stop in Okeechobee, but to my horror just a couple of hundred metres on from the gate the sealed surface gave way to pebbles and another gate blocked the trail. My new friend from the Florida DEP had luckily followed me for this section, unlocked the gate then drove on down the battered trail ahead of me, promising to open any further gates. 'I've not been down here for a long time,' he shrugged. I dared not ask him whether the path improved. Riding Priscilla in off-road conditions other than well-compacted dirt meant that she'd sink into any soft spots, necessitating a lift out of trouble. For the next two hours the path did nothing but decrease in quality, and apart from a brief snack break by a small pond in which a couple of medium sized alligators drifted around, I was operating at full capacity, very much looking forward to bed that night.

Dale Sanders had been in regular contact since we last saw each other on the day of the crash outside Memphis, and it happened that his sister Judi owned a trailer in a park by Lake Okeechobee. She had gone north for the warmer months and like most Florida snowbirds would return when temperatures increased, but she was more than happy to let me kip in her fixed caravan and in turn I was more than happy to accept her offer. I crashed early that night, utterly exhausted from the afternoon's efforts, but not before I dropped Google a note to remove the bicycle trail status from the foul path that had occupied me for so many of the day's hours.

Just across the road from the Summer Breeze trailer park was the Herbert Hoover Dike, which looms 30 feet above Lake Okeechobee to help protect the surrounding lands from potential flooding. Much to my excitement, my map (and a double check on Google's satellite view to confirm) showed a sealed cycle trail around the eastern circumference of the lake, right on top of the dike wall. Although I'd be susceptible to winds the promise of 40 miles of path without traffic was mouthwatering. I was now drawing close to Miami and every inch of the remaining 150 miles that I could make away from main highways was valuable. The danger of being struck by a vehicle always existed, and it didn't matter that I'd survived without incident for 850 miles and over three weeks, these last few days were critical. I was devastated, therefore, when just a few hundred metres along the path I was faced with another gate and no way past. I called my contact from the day before and out he came with a group of people from the South Florida Water Board, all who seemed keen to help, as well as have a gawk at the Bikecar.

A few phone calls were made, keys tried and shoulders shrugged before I was informed that there were so many gates in place around the dike that although I could be let through this one I'd just find myself stuck at the next. 'You have to find another way round,' the party leader told me. I was bitterly disappointed but accepted there was no alternative. The gates were in place to stop motorised vehicles but my predicament had risen other, more critical problems. Nobody seemed to know who was in charge of each section of the path, or where the appropriate keys or access points were.

There were narrow gaps in between the bollards for normal cyclists and pedestrians, several of which had passed us already that morning, what if one of them had an accident or medical emergency up there on the path? No ambulance would be able to gain access, there were no signs saying who to call in the event of an incident, the whole thing was a shambles. Still, I was left with no choice other than to about turn and make my way around the lake. It became a tough day riddled with headwinds, but the challenge was balanced with excitement by a descent into the Everglades. Soon enough, trailers passed me every so often with an airboat on the back, their enormous fans slowly rotating in the wind. I stopped at a small store to find several large alligator skulls resting on the counter and on top of the beer fridge. 'Killed every one of them myself,' said the store owner proudly, a tanned, tattooed man with ripped off denim sleeves.

'With your hands?' I asked, wide eyed.

'Nope, sniper rifle,' he grunted, which was distinctly less impressive.

This was a totally different part of the world from anywhere I'd been through before. A chain gang stopped their work in a ditch as I rode by, and just as I started to think the silence, swinging shovels and steely stares signalled a vast degree of trouble they downed their weapons and started to applaud and wolf whistle. From what I'd seen in films that kind of behaviour might have them locked in The Hole for a few days, but it was a better plight than an all-out attack from a group of prisoners. Before the town of Moore Haven I crossed a bridge only to see an enormous alligator swimming purposefully towards a riverside picnic place. It was huge! I backed up and crashed down a slope into the park, hoping to get a photo of…oh, I don't know…an alligator riding the Bikecar. Sadly the brute seemed unwilling to come too close, which wasn't such a bad thing as it was easily 14 foot long, I'd never grow tired of seeing such wonderful beasts roaming free.

I wouldn't know it until watching some television later that night, but a tropical storm had been approaching all day, the early winds of which battered me for the final two hours of the day on a very pretty but frustratingly indirect road through high cornfields. Buoyed by passing the first road sign of the journey with *Miami* written on it, eventually I reached Clewiston, Florida, which laid claim to the title of 'America's Sweetest Town,' although this seemed like a stretch.

Just about the most amazing thing in amongst the stereotypical commercialism of America was a small alligator swimming through a roadside sewage drain. I didn't fancy sleeping rough beside sewage, alligators or McDonalds, so treated myself to an incredibly sweet night's sleep in a Best Western, but not before using two bike locks to disable Priscilla's front and rear wheels. You never can be too careful.

It was pretty much a straight shot from Clewiston. Well, that's if I didn't take into account another gate. Highway 27 was a rampaging torrent of vehicles but the old highway, just a few hundred metres parallel, appeared to be silent as I pedalled along, overjoyed. Until the gate appeared. Like the ones around Lake Okeechobee this one had a space through which pedestrians could pass but nothing to grace easy progress for a Bikecar. As I approached an old hillbilly with knotted hair and skin like a rhino watched me, his right hand twitching near the pistol wedged into the waist of his ripped jeans. Beside him a miniscule dog yapped on a lead. It's almost as though God knows these journeys should be riddled with tests; as soon as something annoying happens there always appears to be a small dog nearby, compounding the problem. The pup's owner didn't seem too keen to help although eventually, begrudgingly, he suggested that he might know who had the key.

As he wandered off into the distance I considered the horrible thought of retracing the last five miles to rejoin the main highway, then decided to test out some brute strength, of which I usually possess little. I emptied out the storage box and lifted Priscilla's front wheels up and over the bollards, which were then able to rest either side of her narrower midriff. The next part was tricky, with the main weight of the Bikecar biased towards the rear I had to lift close to 120kg directly up, then nudge her forwards, wiggling side to side to allow the wheels past the gate.

Finally, with a scream reminiscent of one of those World's Strongest Men on Boxing Day when they've just managed to loft a pointless round boulder above a vein-dominated head, I heaved the final inches forwards and laid Priscilla down on the right side of the barrier. Yes! The next few miles of road surface was broken up but I cared not and skirted one remaining gate by careering down a grassy bank into a corn field, this time under a modicum of control.

At the town of Belle Glade, Highway 27 plummets south-southeast to eventually become the borderline between the City of Miami and the Everglades. That day out of Clewiston was nothing but a quick stop for supplies in Belle Glade – where my scruffy self was looked up and down with suspicion by the gas station assistant, who charmingly asked if he could check my bag - and then a thick, perfectly straight highway.

My tunnel vision bounced between the wing mirror and the road ahead, feeling a steady build-up of emotion as the miles dripped by, keeping Em posted on my progress by text, using her as my focus, my reason to stay safe and keep pedalling. I couldn't wait to see her. Although I'd thoroughly loved much of the journey she had been by my side and in my pocket, sharing everything. I knew the approach into Miami was going to be the most difficult section of the trip and owed it to Em to maintain concentration and ensure I got to her place smoothly and safely. This, more than the numerical success of the mission, became my priority.

I spent the last night of the journey camped a few metres off the highway on a service road, sheltered from the view of approaching traffic by vegetation that rose up from the swamps either side of my raised platform. Although large, well-worn tracks and holes through the bushes suggested that alligators frequently crossed this roadway from pool to pool I felt strangely safe within my

Sky Tent, separated from the outside world just by a micro thin mesh.

I slept soundly enough and skipped around upon waking, revelling in the moment. *This was it, this was the day.* I could smell Miami. It was smoky, hot and inviting. Wide canals now bordered the highway and I saw ten, maybe fifteen alligators gliding along that morning, just metres from the road. Sadly a baby gator, just a foot long, had squeezed through the protective fence between highway and water and found itself beneath a wheel, its lower jaw ripped back in a final, horrendous scream of death. Rather than become desensitised to the frequent sight of dead animals, instead it sharpened my urge to survive. After all, I was at risk of the same fate. I hadn't kept an exact count, but this was the first alligator on a list including birds, snakes, deer, frogs, rabbits and dogs. Turkey vultures were a regular sight on the verge, cleaning up the sad collateral damage of human civilization

A car pulled up behind me and I instantly remembered a message I'd received two days earlier, from the father of a guy who had followed my Mississippi paddle. Bill Mestrezat had proposed that he come and join me on the Bikecar for a stretch, and here he was having driven across the State from Sarasota, FL. He trailed me in the car for a couple of miles until an airboat tour company appeared on the left, and we crossed the highway to work out a plan in the parking lot. Bill was alone but he had brought his bicycle, which we managed to tie onto the top of the Bikecar. He would ride with me for a while and when ready, detach the bike and cycle back to his car. We certainly looked the part once everything was in place; me with my mountain beard, a 60 year-old bloke who looked fitter than I did, and then our two-tier bike-on-Bikecar combination. It was great!

Bill got into the rhythm quickly and proved good company, his lust for life and fitness balanced by a quiet-spoken nature. In many ways he was the perfect companion, he didn't talk too much and just got on with the job, placing a great deal of trust in me to steer us as the traffic density picked up south of the 75 Freeway. We were now less than 20 miles from the Miami CBD as the crow flies but had a bit of a roundabout circuit to enjoy before the final stretch into town.

For some mind blowing reason the 27 had now been downsized to a one-lane road, which slowed our progress and forced plenty of time on the grass. Then, all of a sudden, there was a short squeal of brakes and a dramatic crunch. Bill and I hunched forwards with the impact although almost instantly it became apparent that we hadn't been struck. Instead, one vehicle was off the road to our right and still rolling into the alligator fence, and a minivan, which seemed to have caused the crash, was directly behind us with a crumpled nose and smoke rising from the damage.

Bill and I looked at each other, trying to work out what had happened. We'd been almost fully off the road at all times, not encroaching on the lane at all. We waited a moment and then I walked over to the scene, where I appeared to be surplus to requirements. The car that had been struck from behind had evidently slowed down and the driver seemed sheepish, but this could have been due to his irate girlfriend who seemed to hold him accountable for everything. Of course, it's always the vehicle behind to blame. I was amazed that that it had taken this long to see such a shunt occurring such was the local tendency to snuggle up to the car ahead. It slowly transpired that the car had slowed in order to get a better look – and perhaps a photo, although I couldn't be sure – of our unique pedal car, and the minivan had been trailing too close to react. Despite this, I was worried about getting brought into the situation. The United States is so grossly litigious I didn't trust that justice would be simple and I wanted to avoid any official part of the case, especially as we hadn't been at fault. Nobody had spoken to me for a while so I returned to the Bikecar and chatted to Bill, and we both decided to push on.

A couple of minutes later a passing car hailed us and pointed back down the road, where a young man was sprinting after us. We stopped and I got up to talk to the guy, who was Hispanic in origin and didn't have much English. It took a while to get the gist of exactly what he was saying but it clearly involved the words 'police'. He wanted us to return to the site of the crash but I refused on safety grounds, wanting to get off the highway as quickly as possible. I told him with a beating heart that we'd wait where we were until the police arrived and then Bill and I endured an uncomfortable half an hour until a horn beeped and the occupants of a car with a big dent in the rear passed, waving happily. That gave us the signal and although the minivan was still stationary several hundred metres back we decided to make a dash for it and escape the horrid scenario once and for all.

Before too long Highway 27 took a 45 degree left turn and made a beeline towards the high rise business district of Miami. The city was right there at the end of the road, still some distance away and obscured partly by smog, but this was visual confirmation of the finish line. Twice before I'd enjoyed a similar experience. Most recently my friend Seb and I caught a glimpse of Las Vegas rising out of the desert after riding from Canada on our tandem bike, but it was my first continental journey that stuck firm in the memory. In mid January 2007, having travelled a great distance overland by skateboard, the imminent end of my journey was marked by a set of skyscrapers. On that occasion they belonged to Brisbane, Australia. I'd been skateboarding for five months, and I was still left to experience my first real fall of the journey - at a bone jarring 40 kmph. I hoped no such incidents waited on this final leg into Miami.

25

Miami

Bill left me after a celebratory Burger King, a meal fit for endurance champions. He clipped his bike together before a final, farewell hug. He'd ridden over 30 miles with me, a larger contribution than anyone else on the trip, and now he had the same distance again to look forward to, albeit back along the same route on his much faster road bike. Priscilla and I were left to meander the back streets of Miami, rounding the airport and taking a slightly more convoluted route than necessary in order to let my distance accumulate towards that magical figure: 1,000.

Em's house was in the district of Coconut Grove south of the centre, and my final big challenge was to reach those silent, beautiful backstreets by crossing Highway 1, otherwise known as the South Dixie. As I approached a junction that crossed directly over the Dixie my GPS counted upwards and I chanted aloud with it, 'Nine hundred and ninety nine point eight! Nine hundred and ninety nine point nine! And…wait for it, one thousand miles! You beauty!'

Things almost ended badly, though. It was carnage on the Dixie and after ten minutes the first opening appeared from both directions. So focused was I on finding space between other vehicles that I didn't see a low navigation curb designed to filter traffic out of the main lanes into a turning position and I overshot my steering, running straight into the curb and bouncing back into the middle of the highway. Three lanes-worth of speeding vehicles were bearing down on me and I had two choices, stare at them and savour every one of my remaining few seconds, or try and reverse the still backwards roll of the Bikecar and move it forwards to some kind of safety in the turning lane.

Within a whisker I managed it and was thankful to see that the cars on the other side of the highway had recognised my predicament and had slowed sufficiently to allow me time to manoeuver around the curb and shoot across to safety. 'Blimey, that was a little too close for comfort,' I said out loud once on the other side, feeling sweat pour in a torrent over my brow, down the bridge of my nose and into a thick, grimy beard.

Coconut Grove was a peaceful paradise, my haven. I didn't see another vehicle on those close, quiet neighbourhood roads. Iguanas scuttled and peacocks strutted alongside luscious tropical trees and plants, which wrapped protectively around every quaint property. I paused at a crossroads as two couples walked in front of me with their dogs. They looked at me in amazement and I told them my brief story. One of the guys introduced himself as Miguel and said he'd always wanted to pedal up the east coast to New York. My answer was simple, 'Dude, you should! If you need any advice drop me a line.' I dug a card out from the bag beside me, handed it over and wished them all a good day.

Up until that moment I'd put no thought at all into where I'd finish. The brief consideration of finding a big, neon Miami sign crossed my mind but such a show wasn't necessary. Although I'd shared shreds of the past month online this journey had been for soul food and it needed no fanfare or ticker tape. I pulled onto Bayshore Drive, the last road before the land emptied into Biscayne Bay and the Atlantic Ocean, and realised that a journey so dominated by motorised transport deserved only one conclusion. I took a right off Bayshore and pulled into a crowded car park, found a space that no average car would fit into and made it my own, then pulled on the brake for a final time.

We were still. I stayed there for minutes, not aware of the mild rush of cars along the road in front of me or of the steady stream of people behind who filtered from the lot into the David T Kennedy Park. The only sound was music. Across the road a wedding was taking place and the choir welcomed my arrival with perfect timing…

When I wake up in the morning, love
And the sunlight hurts my eyes
And something without warning, love
Bears heavy on my mind

Then I look at you
And the world's alright with me
Just one look at you
And I know it's gonna be
A lovely day
Lovely day…
lovely day…
lovely day…
lovely day…

26

The Grove

Her face glowed as we rushed towards each other, that gorgeous smile widening by the millisecond, blonde locks falling in gentle waves over her shoulders. My hands slipped under her arms and around her waist, pulled her nearer, our lips meeting instinctively, all the pent up stress of recent weeks releasing in sighs and affection.

'I love you,' I purred, running my fingers through her hair.

'I love you, too,' Em replied, her blue eyes staring up at me, all mine, making every moment from the past month worthwhile.

*   *   *

I had allowed no time limit to confine the scope of this adventure, instead falling prey to the inclinations of my mind and the strength or weaknesses of my body. I had travelled just as I tried to experience the rest of my life, by living according to how I felt rather than what was expected of me. Any urgency introduced to this challenge - except for the small sprints and swerves necessitated by survival instinct in the face of speeding vehicles - came purely from my heart as I drove towards Miami and the girl I'd been slowly, patiently falling for.

There had been no post expedition blues after The Sail and there were certainly none once my time on a Bikecar had come to an end. Em provided all the consistency I needed to level straight out after such a period of ever-changing vibrancy, as well as the support, friendship and inspiration to fuel whichever next step was brewing. By escaping from the mundane responsibilities and habits that diluted the spirit of my younger self, the subsequent path eventually led to me confronting every aspect of my life.

It had taken some time to accept that I did not fit into a conventional world that used to be presented as the only option for adulthood, but now I knew I could only fully move away from it by allowing myself to have a purpose far removed from that former lifestyle. I now lived to overcome my fears and to challenge myself, with no excuses getting in the way.

There had been endless caution from people I'd met on

the road when I told them Miami was my destination. 'You don't want to go there,' they said, 'there are gangs, guns, Cubans.' My dismissal of these stereotypes just encouraged more visceral persuasion techniques, 'No! Listen! You should not go to Miami. They are crazy down there. They'll kill you!' It just seemed like another version of Comfortable Human Syndrome, there's always an excuse not to go to a place you haven't been or to do something you haven't done. Fear is so striking from a distance but the key is to understand this and not let it hold you back. As my friend Rod Wellington says, 'I carry a lot of things in my kayak, but your fear is not one of them.'

Perhaps though, the Miami-haters had a teeny weeny point. The morning after I arrived the media was dominated by a horrifying story: a mind-altering drug strangely known as Bath Salts seemed to have compelled a man younger than myself to remove all of his clothes and proceed to literally eat another man's face. Such bizarre tales have the potential to imprint upon the reputation of a place, but Em and I decided to see Miami from our own perspective. One, that at the time, only we were privileged enough to enjoy. We hopped onto Priscilla and took a ride through Coconut Grove, a few minutes later ordering lunch at a McDonalds' Drive Thru, the delighted kiosk attendants celebrating our oddness with a lovely dance. 'Is this extra?' I checked with them, just in case there was some local tip-inducing custom we hadn't been told about.

One month had passed since that car hit Rod and I off the road and an inconceivable amount had happened in that time, but the four weeks were now embedded in my memory. The early stages of the Bikecar expedition presented me with the most physically difficult challenge I'd ever encountered, but it is the mental battle and the necessity for focus that will forever define this journey for me. Without doubt, it was the most dangerous challenge of my life and little will usurp that accolade in the years to come. To survive the crash on Day One without any repercussions more serious than a sore shoulder was beyond fortunate, but that encounter certainly clarified what it would take to complete this traverse of the South. When you have a crash it's wise not to react too quickly. Take a moment to work out what's right and what's wrong, then get yourself back on track whatever it takes (the easiest option is usually the wrong one).

It had been a hard expedition, but a rich one. New friends, hours of thinking-time, experiences I wouldn't have ever dreamed of having had I opted for my original plan for April and May – to spend that time writing in a London apartment. It was certainly much cheaper to ride across America! Despite the daily dangers I have grown, I have had fun. I have ridden past armadillos and eagles and snakes and alligators and wild hogs. I have woken to misty mornings and fought through the boiling midday sun. I've felt the face-melting pleasure of a long downhill and the unavoidable frustration of yet another steep climb. The joys of finding the peace of a bicycle path, a quiet state road or even a remote dirt track through the woods became an integral part of my day. I have listened to people tell me I have a death-wish and replied that to the contrary I am riding for the sake of living, with every drop of time and energy I can muster. Sure, there were dangers, but the decision not to finish my Bikecar career immediately after that accident one month earlier was one of the best I ever made. It taught me to embrace the potential for failure as a positive.

In many ways those 1,000.3 miles had painted the perfect representation of everything I'd previously expected of America. The crazy driving, ridiculous opulence, devastating poverty, wide open skies, guns, enormous country, expansive waistlines and capacious hearts. The journey did what any good adventure should do and eradicated the things I usually took for granted. Oh, to delight in the glorious pursuit of finding some flushless place to poo in the great outdoors or the picking of a quiet spot to sleep undiscovered. The endless kindness of strangers met along the way rebuilt trust in the innate goodness of my fellow humans – such decency is rarely buried deep, we just need to sift the soil a little.

Travelling by Bikecar was about facing the possibility of death constantly but continuing, because every day there was a visual, human and sentimental validation of my career and life choices, bonded by my eagerness to reach Miami because Em was there. Of all my expeditions, this one made the most sense to me, regardless of mode of transport or geographical location or intention or reason, because I had a person and not a destination waiting at the end. To meet a girl who was as willing to travel to me as I was to her, someone so innately positive and reasonable and ambitious that she made me want to improve myself, it tied my loose ends together and helped define a clearer sense of my future.

I am reminded not to stop living my life just in case something bad might happen because dreams are best when experienced awake, they shouldn't be locked away until you sleep. To face a challenge can do nothing but make us stronger, and my time with Priscilla left me a better man. No doubt there are many personal flaws to be discovered and lessons to be learned - or worse, forced -

but my caution had again been overcome by optimism, which watered a tiny seed that grew solidly into a big journey between two cities that began with the same letter, and once again thankfully involved absolutely no punctures to speak of.

What would come next wasn't entirely clear but that didn't matter much. All I knew was that everything I needed was right beside me in Miami, and that when the time came for a new adventure the rules were simple: it just needed to offer a fresh test, something new, something difficult, and something that would stretch me out in body and mind, leaving room to fit more inside.

The End

Epilogue

After leaving Miami, Dave went back to the UK and promptly moved out of his flat. Two months later he began what turned out to be the most difficult venture of his life, a 1001 mile swim down the Missouri River between Chamberlain, South Dakota and St Louis, Missouri.

Between May and June 2013 Dave completed the eighth journey of Expedition1000 by riding an ElliptiGO elliptical bicycle from the UK to France. Sadly a canal towpath in Northamptonshire stole away Dave's record of never getting a puncture, mainly because he accidentally ran into a hawthorn hedge and got fifteen in one go.

At the time of publishing he isn't sure what comes next, it's just a waiting game until the next seed comes along. Seventeen thousand-plus milers to go. Won't take long.

Tweets from the
Bikecar journey

'Can you say "I love you"' Girl very intrigued by the English
accent. My reply: 'You'll have to work harder than that'
Apr 16th, 2012

'Anything becomes simple if you understand it.'
- Dale Sanders, Memphis River Rat
Apr 17th, 2012

I should have started Expedition No.6 today. Sadly, the Bikecar
is AWOL. Starting to research other options for travel!
Apr 20th, 2012

If anyone from the #Memphis area happens to have a pogo
stick, a trike, a Big Wheel, a Space Hopper, something like that,
let me know!
Apr 21st, 2012

Time for bed. Up early to start another expedition. Memphis to
Miami on a Bikecar, here we go!
Apr 23rd, 2012

I suppose if a speeding vehicle knocks a #bikecar off the road
it's fitting to end up in a field of corn
Apr 24th, 2012

A 50 year-old man was just told he couldn't pedal
the #bikecar with me, by his Mum
Apr 30th, 2012

A cricket just bounced off the front of a truck into my lap. I
guess that's about as exciting as cricket gets #bikecar
May 1st, 2012

Now, I'd like your honest opinion.
Will anyone take incredible umbrage if I include in my next
video a small segment about midgets?
May 4th, 2012

Good solid morning of #Bikecar'ing. Time for lunch, a snooze
and no doubt at least 25 insect bites
May 4th, 2012

At some point tomorrow I'll enter Alabama and then, Mr
Forrest Gump, you might meet your match...
May 5th, 2013

155.3 miles on the #Bikecar. Chased by 38 dogs.
1 emu. 7 dead snakes. 6 live ones.
2 churches camped at. Mosquitos: 17,325
May 5th, 2012

'That's awesome man.
With these gas prices that's the future right there.'
#ManlooksatBikecar
May 5th, 2012

Very odd campsite, made all the more weird by a hyperactive
bug imitating my mobile phone text alert #bikecar
May 6th, 2012

I'm having breakfast in a place where they're having a farewell
tour for a T-Bone steak. It's hard not to love America
#WaffleHouse
May 7th, 2012

I am quite sure The Wire casting panel found their ghetto rats by
hanging out in Pensacola. #gangstastereotyping
May 7th, 2012

@estesc Just found out my mother -in-law put @DaveCorn up
for a night. You never know when adventure will show up in life
May 8th, 2012

Gorgeous morning. White dunes and beaches to both sides, a
pod of dolphins 30metres offshore, bliss
May 8th, 2012

Just went swimming.
Then someone said they caught a Great White here recently.
I told them it was probably a good time to go swimming.
May 8th, 2012

3 counts of road rage today, 2 from Porsche drivers.
Compensating for something, chaps? #bikecar
May 10th, 2012

Dodged 6000 cars, tick. Spotted 3 manta rays, tick. 1 free lunch,
tick. Crossed 3 bridges, tick.
Made camp, tick. Checked for tics, tick
May 11th, 2012

25mph headwind, day-long thunderstorm, heavy logging traffic
and a partridge in a pear tree. Good morning Florida!
May 12th, 2012

When picking a rest day location try not to go for the town with
a pulp mill, and therefore the permanent smell of cabbage.
May 14th, 2012

Yep, this place still smells like cabbage. Although the locals say it
smells like money. Need to work on your PR, Perry.
May 14th, 2012

110 miles in two days and I'm walking like an oldie! Achilles
tendon flared up, thighs burning. I love it! I'm alive!
May 17th, 2012

Traffic doesn't 'alf ramp up as 10.30am on a Sunday approaches.
Thank you Lord for this extra time in the roadside ditch.
May 20th, 2012

Just interrupted halfway through an interview with National
Geographic Radio by a bunch of reprobates
May 21st, 2012

Blow me down that was a tough day. I look like I've been at sea
for a year. 144 miles left to Miami is the reward, splendid!
May 23rd, 2012

That moment when you just spent your last cash dollar and the
ATM machine rejects your card...grass for dinner, then...
May 25th, 2012

You know you're looking good when gas station attendants ask
to check your bag for stolen goods. #beardjudgment
May 25th, 2012

Sun is overhead, wind is at my tail. If there wasn't a truck every
ten seconds this would be perfect!
May 25th, 2012

Wish I could share the frog and toad orchestra performing in
this Everglades swamp. Dead of night.
Like 1000 old men laughing
May 26th, 2012

I'm going to miss this morning view. Mosquito net, sunrise,
Bikecar. 50 miles left, Miami here I come!
May 26th, 2012

Small bump behind us. We were off the road but as usual cars
driving too close to each other. No damage. Onwards!
May 26th, 2012

Lovely feeling waking up in Miami knowing I don't have to look
in a broken wing mirror today! 1000 miles, and out! #bikecar
May 27th, 2012

Where they are now?

Some time has now passed since the events of this book. Here are some inspirational stories from some of the people featured in these pages.

In addition to her role with Pangaea Explorations and working on personal art projects, **Emily Penn** has spent several months sailing in the Pacific, developing zero waste proposals for remote island communities.

Website: www.emilypenn.co.uk

Rod Wellington kayaked for eight months becoming the first North American to descend the 3800-mile length of the Mississippi Missouri waterway. Despite a grueling winter, he's still smiling.

Website: www.zeroemissionsexpeditions.com

Paul Everitt had a wonderful journey down the Upper Mississippi on an old school raft. He's now planning to kayak around the Mediterranean Sea.

Website: www.going-solo.co.uk

Miguel Endara, the chap who Dave met right at the end of the Bikecar journey, ended up joining the Swim1000 expedition and made an incredible film about that journey. Miguel continues to create groundbreaking art and film.
Website: www.miguelendara.com

Dale Sanders, 78, continues to lead paddling groups along the Wolf River and showed his face at the beginning and end of Swim1000. He's just bought a new canoe, which suggests a bigger trip of his own could be on the way. He's still smiling, too.
Website: www.dalesanders.zenfolio.com

Tommy and **Mary Cornthwaite Winger** now have eleven Chihuahuas

Tim McCarley, **Wayne Pratt et al** hosted another successful Bluz Cruz marathon down the Mississippi. Tim and **K.K** once again excelled in the tandem race.
Website: www.bluzcruz.com

Sean Conway cycled another 16,000 miles around the world after getting hit by a truck and fracturing his spine. In 2013 he plans to swim the length of Britain.
Website: www.seanconway.com

Sarah Outen finally rowed out of Japan but a few weeks later got munched by a storm and required a traumatic rescue. At the time of publishing she was back out in the Pacific, having another go in her new boat, Happy Socks. Website: www.sarahouten.com

Al Humphreys was voted one of National Geographic's adventurers of the year in 2012 and balanced out a series of Microadventures with some much larger challenges, including rowing across the Atlantic Ocean and dragging a cart across Oman's Empty Quarter with another top adventurer, Leon McCarron.
Website: www.alastairhumphreys.com

Follow Dave's Adventures

Official Website: www.davecornthwaite.com

Twitter: @DaveCorn

Facebook: /davecornthwaite & /expedition1000

YouTube: /DaveCornthwaite

Watch Miguel Endara's beautiful short film about Dave's Missouri River swim @ www.swim1000film.com

Thank You

I couldn't possibly live the way I do without the support of others. To a great degree most of us are able to take charge of our own destiny but life is made richer by love, friendship and kindness from both friends and strangers. There are so many people to thank I'm quite sure I'll accidentally omit someone. Forgive me in advance.

To my sponsors, your generosity is inspiring and means I never have to buy clothes: Dave Summers and DMS. Tim, Andy and the cracking crew at Aquapac – I'm sorry you get so many sponsor requests because of me! Dave Gordon and Nic at BAM Bamboo Clothing. Sarah Gowans and the team at Buff. Roger, Lucy and Paul at Nite Watches. Conrad, Vicki and Teresa at the Blue Project. Dov at Hammock Bliss. Dimco. Planet Bike. Natural Hero, Palm Equipment Europe, Cushe Footwear and the awesome team at Powertraveller.

A special thanks to Jo Hill, who has provided a home to me whenever I've been in London, except for that ill-fated time when I decided to try having a flat of my own. I'm not sure that the 42" telly from Swansea quite repays the debt I owe you.

Paul Everitt, for planting a seed that made a wonderful journey possible. I still don't know how anybody can be clever enough to build something like Priscilla, but you are. Thank you.

Rod Wellington, your own achievements astound me, yet you still have time to offer true friendship and that most valuable of gifts, time itself.

Henrietta Atkinson, (Big Tall) Jake Lindgren, Liz Froment, Oli Milroy and Louis Bedwell; when I set up the Adventure Internship I had no idea I'd meet such wonderful people (although we haven't actually met, Liz, we may as well have!) that could have such an impact on my work. You're all stars.

To everyone on board Sea Dragon for the wonderful company and discussion. When's the next one? Danny Loo, Andrew Cook, Monica Varadan, Natalia Cohen, Nicola Moss, Davin Luoma, Tina Beck, Jesper Mortensen and Dale Selvham. Eddie Kisfaludy for getting us to Cabo in the first place. Sara Close and Seth Warren for your hospitality. Kahi Pacarro, Louise Shinkoethe Pacarro, Tristan Sea, Aaron Rosenblatt, Lindsey Ka'imi Kesel and Jess Rohr for the Hawaii welcome.

To my Memphis crew. Dale and Meriam Sanders, Rachel Sumner, Jonathan Brown, Tom Roehm, Richard Sojourner, Jeff and Eileen Sojourner, Mike Watson, Boyd and Lucy Wade, Linda Weghorst, Mary Finlay, Roger Graham, Ken Kimble, Richard and Judy Day, Sandy Stacks, Keith Cole, Anna Hogan, Genny Kilpatrick, Jamie Zelazny and finally, JJ the rooster from Millington Store, TN. (Sadly, JJ passed away after twenty years of terrorising the locals).

To the kind and generous once-strangers-now-friends on the road between Memphis and Miami. Tim, Cindy, K.K and Julia McCarley. Wayne Pratt. Aaron Sackler and the staff at Sacks Outdoors in Hattiesburg, MS. Rusty Easterling and family at the Black Creek Cabin, MS. Gareth and Rhi Williams. Dana Robertson and Nick Kinderman. Terri Johnson. Bruce and Lisa Common. Leslie, Kent, Maddie and Olivia Kolovich. Joan Vienot. Gabriel Gray. Bill Oestreich and all the staff at Bird's Underwater Dive Shop in Crystal River, FL. Dick and the pedalling crew in Floral City, FL. Boyd and Justin from the National Geographic Weekend Radio Show. Mary Cornthwaite Winger, Tommy Winger and all their animals, even the small dogs. Bill Mestrezat and Miguel Endara.

And to everyone else who had a small hand to play in this book and the story behind it. John Ruskey, Carrie Formosa, Cristina Vigo, Rachel Morrison, David Clarke, Sean Conway, Sarah Outen, Alastair Humphreys, Clair Maurice, Sara Salo, Katherine Avery and Hazel Mansfield.

Kris and Maren Hallenga and all their boobettes; endless motivation and inspiration for boob lovers everywhere! Please visit and support www.coppafeel.org

Victor & Sergio, for being total legends and letting me spend two months writing this book in El Ultimo Mono Juice and Coffee in Malaga, Spain. Love you guys.

My Mum and Dad, brother Andy and sister-to-be Maddy. You've always been there, always supportive despite the crazy ideas. Couldn't do this without you.

And finally, Emily Penn. You make me want to better myself and I'm stronger for knowing you. Much of the philosophy in this book we developed together, or you brought it into my life afresh. Life is pretty good alone, but it's immensely epic when shared. Thank you for everything lovely one, keep those blue eyes shining please.

If you enjoyed this book, please do leave a review on Amazon.com (or.co.uk), it'll help other people decide to buy it (or not!).

And remember, if you're ever lacking in motivation, the best way to get yourself out of a rut is to combine three simple words.

www.sayyesmore.com

Now, off you go and have an adventure.

Goodbye for now.

Dave

Printed in Great Britain
by Amazon.co.uk, Ltd.,
Marston Gate.